Solo Suppers

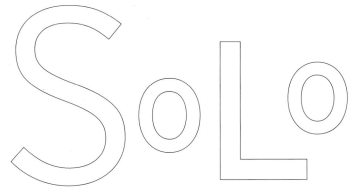

SoLo
Suppers

Simple Delicious Meals
to Cook for Yourself

Joyce Goldstein

Photographs by Judi Swinks

CHRONICLE BOOKS

SAN FRANCISCO

Library of Congress Cataloging-in-Publication Data:
Goldstein, Joyce Esersky.
Solo suppers : simple delicious meals to
cook for yourself / by Joyce Goldstein ;
photographs by Judi Swinks. p. cm.
ISBN 0-8118-3620-7 (pbk.)
1. Suppers. 2. Cookery for one. I. Title.
TX738 .G68 2003
641.5'61−dc21
2002151400

Manufactured in China.

Designed by **Vanessa Dina**
Typesetting by **Janis Reed**
Food and prop stylist **Randy Mon**
Food styling assistant **Allie Liebgott**

Judi Swinks and Randy Mon would like to thank:
Crate and Barrel, Zinc Details, and Frederick Preyer
for generous loan of their props.

Distributed in Canada by Raincoast Books
9050 Shaughnessy Street
Vancouver, British Columbia V6P 6E5

10 9 8 7 6 5 4 3 2 1

Chronicle Books LLC
85 Second Street
San Francisco, California 94105

www.chroniclebooks.com

Joyce Goldstein would like to say Thank You to:

Maureen Lasher, for believing that singles really do cook.
Bill LeBlond, for knowing that singles need good recipes and supporting me all the way. Sharon Silva, copy editor goddess, who has spoiled me for anyone else. Amy Treadwell, for keeping us all on track. Vanessa Dina, for the lovely design of this book. Judi Swinks, for the enticing food photos. Randy Mon, for making the food look real and inviting. Michele Fuller, for her excellent work in getting the word out about *Solo Suppers*. Doralece Dullaghan for encouraging me to teach a class on cooking for one. Ellen Rose, for enthusiastic feedback and random recipe testing. Bruce Aidells, for talking it up. Zanne Stewart of *Gourmet* magazine, for including my recipes in "Dinner for One." Andy Powning, for fascinating vegetable discussions and fine produce. Bill Niman, for fine beef, pork, and lamb and home delivery for special events! Mike Weinberg-Lynn, for fine seafood and home delivery for recipe testing and special events. Evan Goldstein and Doug Fletcher, for wine storage advice. And to my loving family and friends. Because of them, not all of my suppers are solo.

CoNTenTs

Introduction

Singles represent the fastest-growing segment of the U.S. population. In 1940, 8 percent of all American households were made up of singles. Today, more people are living alone than are living in nuclear families. Married couples with children represent 23 percent of the population, while singles are 27 percent and increasing. People live alone for many different reasons: never married, divorced, widowed, left in the "empty nest" when the last of the kids moves out. They are on their own—no roommates, no mate—by choice or by fate. For the most part, they are happy and not lonely. They have friends and family and lead active lives.

Most cookbooks and magazines have not reflected this demographic shift. The average recipe is still designed to serve the nuclear family, with four to six portions. But if you cook for one, you know from frustrating experience that not every recipe reduces easily or well. After doing the math, you often find that there's not enough seasoning or too little liquid. Even the timing may be off. A few cookbooks have been written for the single-person household, but, for the most part, they have been aimed at young singles with little real cooking and dining experience, and often on a tight budget. These books have been friendly and pragmatic, but largely lacking in culinary inspiration. In other words, they certainly wouldn't send me into the kitchen.

There is a growing market of sophisticated single diners who have traveled extensively, dined out in all manner of restaurants, know how to cook, and love to eat well. I am one of those solo diners who doesn't order takeout or cook frozen dinners. You could say I'm a snob, and that's partly right, but the truth is that I know my way around a kitchen and still enjoy being there. Having been a cooking teacher for more than thirty-five years, a restaurant chef for sixteen years, and a single diner for ten years, I have the experience to be able to create delicious and well-thought-out recipes for singles and can offer a personal outlook on how to market for and plan meals with both panache and practicality.

Like many singles, I eat out once or twice a week, occasionally more, usually with friends or business associates, rarely on my own (unless I am traveling). I entertain friends and members of my family about once a week. The rest of the time I eat at home by myself. I am spoiled. I want to eat as well at home as I did when I had a restaurant and ate in the back kitchen or when I cooked for my family every night and showered them with love, attention, and home-cooked meals they still yearn for even today. I want to eat as well as when I entertain friends at home (usually minus the dessert). I believe that I deserve a great meal, a glass of excellent wine, and the time to relax and enjoy my own company. Also, I love to cook.

Why call this book *Solo Suppers* and not *Solo Meals*? Because the evening meal is when eating alone has the most meaning and impact. Eating breakfast without company is no big thing. Even when you live with others, breakfast is rarely a social occasion. You read the paper, grab a muffin or bagel and coffee, and realize that there's not much time to linger at table (except maybe on Sunday, when you can lounge in your bathrobe, with the *New York Times* in one hand, coffee cup in the other, enjoying a lovely morning that may extend to noon or later). Lunch more often than not occurs while you are working. You may eat at your desk or grab a bite near the office, and even if you work at home, it's unlikely that you'll stop to cook because there is too much to do. Again, weekends may be different, but most solo people I know run a zillion errands on Saturday, see friends Saturday night, and on Sunday see friends, family, or films. They might do some cooking on Sunday for the rest of the week, but it's a low-key social day and probably an early evening.

Now, I realize that some people believe that the obvious solution to cooking for one is a book of only fast and easy recipes. They assume that single diners want to get the mealtime over with as quickly as possible. What is implied in this assumption is that cooking for yourself and dining alone is so abhorrent that "cook fast, eat fast, and get it over with" should be the single's way of life. I agree that on many nights a fast and easy meal is just right. But for those of us who love good food, and cooking, there are also many nights when we enjoy spending a bit of time in the kitchen. We're in no rush, there's no pressing engagement. Home is where the heart is, along with the stomach, so it's an ideal time to cook and dine in a leisurely way.

Cooking solo can be both rewarding and creative. First, it allows you the luxury to experiment. You can try dishes that you are not yet ready to cook for others until you are sure the recipes are delicious and worth the effort. Also, while I love soups and stews, the experience of dining endlessly on leftovers can get old fast. I delight in fabulous one-shot dinners, with nary a crumb left over. And I love getting multiple uses out of a basic ingredient. For example, if I cook beets as a vegetable one night, a few nights later I will use the balance in a salad. My meals are often simple, but never simple-minded. Occasionally I am extravagant and self-indulgent. Good for me! Remember that what might be expensive if ordered in a restaurant can be an incredible bargain when you are the chef at home.

Even shopping can be creative. I love wandering through the stalls at the farmers' market, letting the produce inspire my upcoming meals. I like to browse ethnic markets and specialty-food shops at home and abroad, seeking new ingredients to add to my basic pantry. I especially relish improvisational meals assembled from a few fresh ingredients and the backup of my well-stocked pantry. I also enjoy creating new dishes by seeing what's in my refrigerator and pantry and putting them together so they seem new and wonderful, even though some of the parts of the meal were eaten in a different way a few days earlier. Cooking like this can be a creative challenge; it's either a fast game of beat-the-clock or a slow process of both learning and enjoyment. Sometimes I'm in a hurry to catch a movie or go to a play with friends. Sometimes dinner is my play, and I love the adventure of seeing what I can come up with, given what I have on hand and my ability to recognize my true culinary desires for the evening.

Eating is ideally a social activity, best shared with others. But if no others are available, you still have to eat. Take the time to enjoy cooking for yourself and make your evening a pleasant one by reading, listening to music, thinking—whatever it takes for you to relax and appreciate the solitude. The reality for most singles is that while our days may be busy, our work fulfilling, our friends wonderful, and our family beloved and equally busy, we are at home alone many a night and need to eat. *Solo Suppers* is a book for those nights when you don't want to depend on mediocre takeout and can't face one more broiled chicken breast or the same soup for the fourth night in a row. It is a book for when you are alone and want a satisfying home-cooked meal. Of course, it's great to cook for others, too, and there is no reason why some of these recipes cannot be doubled to share with another person. But only if his or her company is as good as your own.

Shopping for One

Cooking for one is easy. Shopping for one is more challenging. In fact, it might be the most difficult part of cooking for yourself. I try to be careful not to let my eyes be bigger than my stomach or refrigerator. The produce at my local farmers' market is so seductive, I tend to get carried away. I hope that the food I buy will last if I should have to go out unexpectedly, because I hate to have to perform a garbage-pail sacrifice, during which I ceaselessly berate myself for wasting food.

When I go to the market, I fall in love with food. I constantly need to remind myself about moderation. Only one basket of berries, please, even if they are three for $4.50. How many kinds of tomatoes can I eat this week? I know they look great on the windowsill, but will I end up throwing away a few because they've spoiled? Reality planning and a modicum of self-discipline is required if you are to avoid waste and guilt.

Before I shop I try to remember to look at my calendar to see if I have time to market a few times during the week or if I must go once and plan for several meals simultaneously. Usually I take a quick inventory of what's in my refrigerator, opening those closed and unmarked containers and playing the mental game of use it or lose it. Inspired in part by the thought of using

some of those leftovers, I may already have a few ideas of what I want to cook or eat, but more often than not I let what I see at the market determine my meals. If my mood changes and I no longer want turnips or kale after I've bought them, I cope and try to become reinspired. Reading cookbooks helps set my creative mind back to the ingredients on hand.

Shopping at a supermarket can be even more difficult than at a farmers' market, where you can usually buy as little as you need. There's the matter of bunches. Yes, I can buy a few loose carrots, rather than a bunch, but those loose carrots are often old and starchy. Yes, I can buy a few loose beets, but their leaves are gone and they are tired looking. So I buy a bunch. I know I can't eat a bunch of either vegetable at a sitting. I could take the time to divide the bunch of beets and cook them twice, but that seems like a poor use of my time. Beets take twenty-five to forty-five minutes to cook, depending on their size. Cooked beets hold quite well for many days, which means that they will have to be revisited in a creative way, reheated as a leftover, or thrown out if I've forgotten about them in the back of the fridge.

And what about those appealing little bunches of herbs? How much tarragon can a person eat without getting tired of its licoricey perfume? Will it keep for more than a week, or will I discard half of it and waste sixty cents? It's the idea of waste more than the money. It would be nice to split the herbs with a friend, but no one else may be in the mood for tarragon or dill. Can I dry them? Preserve them in oil? Make a sauce that will keep for a while? I know a window box or small garden patch is a great idea, but not a realistic option for everyone. So does the solo cook have to give up fresh herbs? Either you may have to learn to live with a little waste, or you will have to become very creative in sauce preparation.

Bunches are just one quandary. What if I am in the mood for roast chicken or meat loaf or, heaven forbid, a rib roast or leg of lamb? Do I have to suppress gratification? Must I ignore my inner cravings and only serve such items when I have company? Should I call around to rustle up a dinner guest to share the meal? Or do I make the chicken or roast anyway and hope I can eat the leftovers and not get sick of them? While not everything can be turned into hash, pasta sauce, risotto, soup, salad, or sandwiches, you'd be surprised at how many variations you can create with leftovers and not feel burdened or bored.

These are some of the culinary decisions a single person must make. While the vast majority of recipes in this book are one-shot meals with no leftovers, there will be a few that address the question of making a whole chicken and using what's left, or planning ahead and cooking two pieces of tuna and using one of them in a pasta or salad within the next few days.

Planning Meals

When you are responsible for cooking for a family, meal planning is important. Others are dependent on you for both sustenance and culinary pleasure. You want to serve balanced meals and offer diverse menus over the course of a week or two. For some, menu planning is an enjoyable creative challenge; for others, it is a difficult or tedious task. Of course, when you cook primarily for yourself, meal planning seems less important. Indeed, some people never do it. They want to feel liberated from such routine or responsibility. They want to be extemporaneous at all costs. Shop, make a meal, eat it, and that's all there is to it. If you are not in the mood to make supper and will settle cheerfully for a bowl of cold cereal, who is to know or care?

Meal planning does not have to be complex, rigid, and routine. It is usually as simple as making a bit more of something so that you have

interesting options for a second meal the next night or even a few days later. While this kind of thinking ahead is not required, it can save time and effort. And I find it fun and inspiring to recycle cooked food in a creative fashion.

When I buy a piece of tuna, I often select a slice that is somewhat larger than a single serving so I can have tuna salad or tuna pasta a few nights later. If my week is unpredictable and I don't know if I'll be home in time to use the leftover tuna before it spoils or tastes tired, I'll buy just enough for one meal. When I cook rice, barley, *farro*, or beans, I sometimes make a double batch so that I have it for another dinner. Having this side dish on hand shortens the cooking time on a night when I need a quick and easy meal. When I am in the mood for meatballs, I generally make enough for two meals, as rolling them can be a pleasurable meditative activity if I have the time, but a nuisance if I am in a hurry. One batch might be eaten with mashed potatoes or polenta. The second time around they could be used in a soup or in a sauce for pasta. And when I make roast chicken just for me, because I am in the mood, I am already anticipating a delicious dinner a night or two down the road.

A NOTE ON PORTION SIZE

The recipes in this book are average-size portions for one. If you are a small eater, some of them may seem large. Many of the recipes represent one-dish meals rather than multiple courses, so I have made them substantial. If you find them too large, cut back or just enjoy the leftovers.

Stocking the Basic Pantry

Setting up a basic pantry is one of the most important tasks of the solo cook. By combining two or three fresh ingredients or leftovers with carefully selected staples that you have on hand, you can have a superb and satisfying supper.

Leftovers: The Basic Reheat and the New Creation

Leftovers fall into two categories. The first is the basic reheat; in other words, you eat it again just as you prepared it the first time. More interesting for the cook is the creative use of leftovers to make a new dish. Fortunately, both kinds of leftovers have a place in your life. If you've made a hearty soup, it is perfectly wonderful reheated, maybe even better. No need to change it. Good is good, even the second time around. (With the advent of the microwave oven, reheating leftovers is a snap.) For a little variety, you can change the side dishes. If you served the stew the first time with rice, try pasta, kasha, *farro,* or potatoes when you reheat it. And on those nights when you are too tired to think about cooking and leftovers are all you can manage, you'll really appreciate your foresight for having made enough for a second helping.

At culinary schools, a big fuss is made over an exercise called "the market basket." The teachers bring identical baskets of ingredients to different chefs and then see what diverse menus and dishes they concoct. And then, because it is a school exercise, they evaluate the results. The solo cook-diner plays this game quite often, and not just with a market basket of fresh ingredients. That's easy. More often you are working with a combination of a few fresh ingredients, leftovers, and basic pantry staples—a greater challenge! Fortunately, the only person you have to please is yourself. If the dish is a disaster or disappointment, if the flavors are muddled or not what you'd imagined, you can always make an omelet, or sip a glass of wine and eat cheese and bread, have a salad, and relax. If the dish you create is not brilliant, but is still good enough to eat, fine. You've dined economically and well. Sometimes you may invent a dish so good you want to take notes and create it again and again. That is part of the adventure of solo cooking. You're free to make a mistake, a middling meal, or a masterpiece.

Leftovers: Basic Reheats

Soups
change the garnish or add a protein

Stews
serve with rice, mashed potatoes, noodles, or polenta

Cooked vegetables
carrots, beets, green beans, asparagus, and so on

Cooked grains
farro, polenta, rice

Cooked beans and legumes
white beans, black beans, chickpeas, lentils

Leftovers: New Creations

Steak use in steak salad

Farro use as salad, reheat as a *farrotto* (with a vegetable), add to soup

Vegetables such as asparagus, beets, green beans, artichokes, and potatoes use in a composed salad, pasta, risotto, soup, or frittata

Salmon or tuna use in a salad or pasta

Chicken use in a salad, soup, pasta, risotto, or sandwich

Shrimp use in a salad, soup, quesadilla, pasta

Rice or couscous use for salad or add to soup

If you have not had time to market and you're too pooped or cranky to shop, you can create a tasty dinner from goodies you have on the cupboard or refrigerator shelf or in the freezer.

One of the most important culinary lessons I learned while living in Italy was that you should always take the time to find the very best ingredients. Some of my Italian friends would drive a half hour out of their way to get sausage made by a particular butcher in the next town, even though a good sausage was available in their own village. One can economize in many ways, and shop the weekly specials at the market, but for the pantry you will want to splurge and get the finest possible ingredients. They often make all the difference between a good meal and a wonderful one.

THE CUPBOARD

Oils: A variety of oils for cooking is a must. Buy in small amounts until you know the oils whose flavor you love. Extra-virgin olive oils vary from a peppery Tuscan oil to an almondy Spanish oil to a fruity California oil, and each will give a different flavor profile to a dish. You may want to splurge on walnut or hazelnut oil for salads or on lemon- or orange-infused oil for salads and cooked vegetables or to spoon over grilled fish. Fine oils are expensive, but are typically worth their cost. A neutral-tasting pure olive oil for making mayonnaise or frying and a bland canola or corn oil for deep-frying should round out the selections. If you do any Asian cooking, add a small bottle of sesame oil. Although many bottles are elegant, please do not use them for stove-top display. Keep oils away from heat and light, preferably in a dark, cool cabinet. Also, try to use the oils rather than collect them as if they were wine. They can go rancid after a year or two. Nut oils, once opened, are best stored in the refrigerator as they turn rancid very quickly.

Vinegars: Yes, it's great to have balsamic vinegar on hand. Market shelves are filled with them,

real ones and those imposters, regular vinegars flavored with caramel. Shop carefully and accept that you must pay more for a quality product. It is in the selection of good red wine and white wine vinegars that the pickings are slimmer. I love a flavorful, wine-scented red wine vinegar for vinaigrettes. I know that sounds funny, but many red wine vinegars have no fragrance or hint of wine and are incredibly harsh and tannic. You may need to sample a few before you find one you like. Champagne vinegar, maybe an aged sherry vinegar, a rice vinegar, a cider vinegar, and an inexpensive distilled white vinegar will round out your pantry, unless you fall in love with a fruit-based vinegar and have room to store it. Vinegars keep quite well.

Soy Sauce: Soy sauce is no longer an exotic ingredient. Many cooks reach for soy instead of salt. If you love Asian-inspired flavors, soy will be an essential part of your pantry. Light soy is less salty and can be used a bit more liberally than regular soy.

Condiments: Most of us have ketchup as a staple. You'd be surprised what a little spritz can do to round out a sauce. Some cooks prefer the texture and taste of chili sauce and spoon it into a marinade. Others like Asian chile pastes. Sample some and keep one or two on hand. Buy the smallest jars possible. We all have a favorite hot sauce that we add to perk up a dish gone flat or in need of a jolt of heat. Pick one or two you like. And maybe a barbecue sauce, too. Many keep well in a cool cupboard, but to be safe, especially if you don't use them often, refrigerate them after opening.

I find that an assortment of mustards provides culinary diversity. A strong Dijon mustard, a whole-grain mustard, and a hot-and-sweet mustard (see page 29 to make your own) will add depth of flavor to sauces and vinaigrettes. The market shelves are packed with flavored mustards. Some are good; some sound creative but in fact are dreadful. Taste and be selective.

Powdered mustard also adds a bit of subtle heat to a dish, so I keep a can on hand.

While I much prefer to grate fresh horseradish with distilled vinegar and store it in the refrigerator, I do occasionally buy a small jar of prepared horseradish. After opening, store it in the refrigerator. It becomes milder over time.

Canned Foods: In the winter, I rely on canned plum tomatoes, diced tomatoes, tomato purée, and even prepared tomato sauce for sauces and stews. Small cans are available. I keep a tube of tomato paste in the refrigerator for the times when a hint of tomato is needed to brighten a sauce. I stock canned chickpeas and white beans and buy small cans of top-quality canned tuna packed in olive oil. (No water-packed tuna for me. I want flavor.) I keep homemade chicken stock in the freezer, but for emergencies I have low-sodium canned broth on hand: chicken, vegetable, and beef. I also keep soup base on the shelf, such as the porcini broth cubes from Knorr that I bring back from Italy whenever I go.

A small can of coconut milk or cream comes in handy for certain Asian soups and curries. I have a small container of capers packed in salt in the pantry, but if you use brined capers, store them in the refrigerator once they are opened, along with oil-packed anchovies. I used to buy those huge cans of salt-packed anchovies, but they take up more room than I am willing to give them. Now the same company is putting out a delicious oil-cured anchovy, and the jar is small.

It's good to have a few jars of olives on hand, for appetizers and snacks and for cooking. These can be doctored up by warming them with herbs, strips of lemon zest and chiles, in a little extra-virgin olive oil. Sometimes I have a jar of bottled grape leaves, too, in case the urge for dolmas strikes.

Dry Staples and Spices: I always store an assortment of dried legumes in jars, including lentils, split peas, cannellini beans, chickpeas, and black beans. They can be added to soups or salads and help stretch a meal.

I also have grains in small amounts: basmati rice, jasmine rice, arborio rice, wild rice, *farro*, polenta, barley, and occasionally bulgur, although it can go rancid quickly. I store these in jars as well, as weevils are known to arrive along with them, and I don't want the pesky bugs taking over my pantry.

An assortment of dried pasta in a variety of shapes is invaluable. Many a night, pasta has been my impromptu dinner, too. Couscous, dried bread crumbs, homemade toasted bread crumbs (page 82), and matzo meal are kept in airtight containers.

Recipe Suggestions: Using Items in the Pantry

Pasta with pesto and potatoes

Pasta with canned tomatoes, olives, capers, and with or without tuna or anchovies

Pasta with garlic, toasted bread crumbs, lemon zest, and tuna

Spaghetti alla carbonara

Risotto with saffron, almonds, and peas

Curried rice pilaf with nuts and dried fruit

Cheese omelet or soufflé

Potato and onion frittata

Grilled cheese sandwich

Quick potato and onion soup

Lentil or bean soup with pasta or rice

Dolmas

Black bean or red bean chili without meat

Any kind of quiche

Bean salad with canned tuna and garlic-oregano vinaigrette

Flour, sugars, baking powders, kosher salt, sea salt, and assorted spices are best stored in a cool, dark cupboard. Spices fade fast, so buy the smallest amounts possible except for those you use all the time, such as peppercorns.

Honey and Preserves: Keep a few jars of honey—lavender, chestnut, citrus blossom—on hand for sweetening sauces, spreading on biscuits, or spooning alongside selected cheeses. I have assorted marmalades, chutneys, and other preserves, although I must confess that most of mine are homemade, as canning is a hobby and a form of relaxation for me.

Dried Fruits, Chocolate, Extracts, and Specialty Condiments: Dried fruits such as raisins, currants, apricots, and prunes come in handy for braising with meats, for desserts, and for noshing. Chocolate, unsweetened cocoa powder, and vanilla and almond extracts are necessary for desserts. Because of my interest in Middle Eastern foods, I have a jar of tahini, a bottle of pomegranate molasses, and rose and orange-flower waters.

Fresh Vegetables: Onions, garlic, shallots, fresh ginger, and potatoes are stored in a cool, dark place in the cupboard. I buy what I need and try to use them within a week or two.

Spirits: While they are not actually in the pantry, I do keep a bottle of Marsala and one of white vermouth in my liquor cabinet for kitchen use. Brandy, ouzo, dark rum, and a few favorite fruit liqueurs join them for occasional use in the kitchen.

THE FREEZER

Some of my basic pantry resides in the small freezer that tops my refrigerator. There are containers of homemade chicken and fish stock. All walnuts, almonds, hazelnuts, and pine nuts are stored in zipped plastic bags, as they can become rancid quickly. To prevent the emergence of weevils, I keep imported porcini and dried ancho and chipotle peppers in the freezer, too.

I have a few carefully wrapped packages of sliced pancetta to enhance pasta sauces and soups or for when the spaghetti alla carbonara craving hits, and maybe a Muscovy duck breast or two. A couple of pounds of unsalted butter are always on hand, and tiny jars of rendered chicken and goose fat are stored in the back of the freezer. I don't use them often, but I know they are there if I need them. A package of frozen peas or corn can come in handy, as can a loaf of bread and a package of English muffins.

THE REFRIGERATOR

I'd be lost without lemons, oranges, and limes, but especially lemons. I use both the zest and the juice in many dishes. They provide the bright flavor accents. As I do a lot of North African cooking, I always have a jar of preserved lemons on hand. Herbs, carrots, and celery are purchased as I need them. I buy the smallest amounts possible.

However, I am not moderate with cheese. It is my weakness. My cheese drawer holds too large an assortment. Most of it is for snacks, desserts, and cooking. I do have a tiny amount of grated pecorino and Parmesan for the occasions when I am in a hurry and don't have time to grate the quantity needed for a dish. But I also have the same cheeses in bulk to grate to order on a bowl of pasta or soup. Cottage cheese, a small container of sour cream, crème fraîche, mascarpone cheese, and yogurt are in the refrigerator, too. A jar of mayonnaise is on hand, in case I haven't made my own, and a jar of peanut butter for my grandchildren and for making peanut sauce. I always have eggs, butter, and sometimes a small container of half-and-half or light cream, milk, or heavy cream.

Outfitting the Kitchen

Far be it from me to tell you what equipment to buy. I am an equipment addict and have collected too much. My rationalization is that because I am a cooking teacher and I am asked to recommend equipment, I need to try all kinds so that I can evaluate their properties. I do cook for large groups from time to time, for my family and friends often, and for myself the most, so I need a diverse assortment. My best advice is to buy only what you really need. Despite all those tempting low-price offers, I do not recommend buying sets of cooking equipment. There will be some pieces that you will use all the time, and then a few that you rarely, if ever, have the occasion to use.

You should have a small sauté pan for omelets and two larger ones for vegetables, meats, and fish (8 inch, 10 inch, and 12 inch are good), and a pot to boil water for pasta and to make stock (4 to 6 quarts). A heavy Dutch oven for stews and braising will come in handy, as will a few small saucepans for sauces, heating up soups, and so on (1 and 2 quarts, plus a small "butter melter"). Don't forget to get the lids, too. I have a wok for stir-frying and deep-frying, a pan that holds a steamer rack for vegetables, a small roasting pan and rack to hold a duck or chicken, a small loaf pan, and heatproof glass dishes and custard cups for gratins and the like. Acquire a few sharp knives and a sharpening steel, a microplane grater, some stainless-steel mixing bowls in assorted sizes, measuring cups and spoons, a colander, a sieve, a couple of baking sheets, whisks, some spatulas and wooden spoons, and a pair of tongs, and you are ready to cook.

For solo cooks, I would recommend getting the smallest food processor, as the big one is too large for many recipes. A mini-processor can be used to grate small amounts of ginger and mince garlic and chiles quickly and efficiently. A blender, a toaster oven, and a microwave oven to thaw stock or reheat leftovers are useful appliances to live on your countertop. A hand mixer or stand mixer is essential if you like to bake.

Keeping Wine

Wine has always been part of my evening meal. I have a small wine cellar, and I buy judiciously whenever the opportunity presents itself. I have some inexpensive house whites and reds for everyday drinking and some wonderful bottles that I serve to friends and family for special meals and to me when I want to celebrate. But when you dine alone and drink a glass or two of wine, how do you take care of the rest of the bottle so the wine doesn't fade quickly or even go bad? There are a few solutions to this dilemma.

First, try to find half bottles. They are the solo diner's friend. The next best bet is to buy a can of wine preservative spray that combines nitrogen and argon gas. I use Private Reserve brand, which is sold in wine stores and liquor shops. A few spritzes of this harmless mixture fills the airspace in the bottle. You can then recork the bottle and it will keep for a few days. My son, Evan, a master sommelier, recommended this solution and also gave me some Champagne resealing tops that keep sparkling wine sparkly for a few days in the refrigerator. Doug Fletcher, a wine maker, had another brilliant suggestion to keep wine alive. He gifted me with three small clear glass bottles with screw tops and told me that as soon as I opened a bottle, I should pour the wine into the screw-top bottles and seal them well. The wine will keep for up to two weeks in the fridge.

If I have opened a bottle of Pinot Noir, I try to plan two nights of meals that work with the wine. Same with Sauvignon Blanc or Chianti. The two nights don't have to be consecutive, but the point of drinking wine with food is to have the two elements harmonize so that the meal is more than the sum of its parts.

The Microwave Oven

I am such an old-fashioned cook that for years I resisted buying a microwave oven. I knew that it was not really an "oven" in the classic sense of the word. Everyone I knew used it to reheat coffee, melt chocolate and butter, thaw frozen dinners, and pop popcorn. I know how easy it is to melt butter and chocolate, and I don't eat frozen dinners, so I didn't really need one. At least, I thought I didn't. One evening when I was at my son's house, I noticed that it took him just seconds to reheat leftovers, and they didn't dry out. When I reheated stews, soups, or leftover vegetables, I would place them in the proper pan and heat them on the stove top very, very carefully or in the oven. It took a long time and sometimes the food suffered. I felt that I had injured my own good cooking. Finally, my daughter convinced me to get a microwave oven for leftovers only. It has changed my life.

I can put vegetables, meat, and grain on one plate and reheat the plate! I can heat pasta or vegetable gratins without drying them beyond palatability. Turkey and stuffing drizzled with gravy are like Thanksgiving at its best. Even rib roast bones remain juicy. I am impressed. I have not yet popped corn or melted butter, but I will confess that I have reheated coffee a few times. Anyway, I am no longer a total culinary snob. Yes, I can cook the long way, the short way, and now I can quickly reheat my good work in the microwave without dirtying all the pots and pans in the house just for one supper.

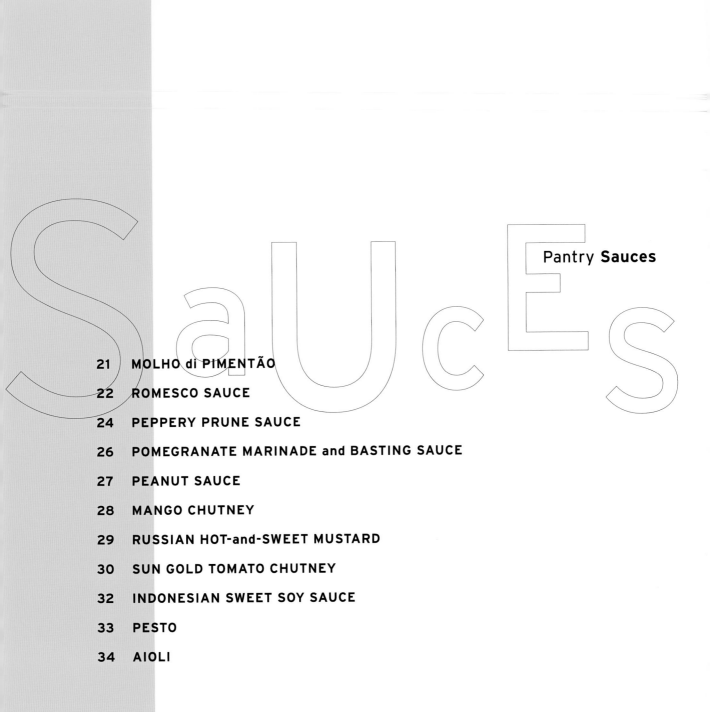

Pantry **Sauces**

Pantry **Sauces**

Today, one can buy all manner of sauces and condiments at the supermarket. The selection is mind-boggling. While I like to sample some of the new items, just to see what's current, ultimately I prefer to make my own. I like to create sauces to suit my personal palate, rather than settle for middle-of-the-road commercial products. Most sauces are easy to prepare, and their versatility will provide you with many pleasurable meals. I keep discovering new ways to use them, and I am still excited by their creative possibilities and variations.

On days when I am in the mood to cook, am enjoying a spurt of creative energy, and have the time, I stock my pantry with an assortment of homemade sauces. I know there will be many busy days ahead, and with these sauces that keep for months, I'll be able to come home and make a quick, delicious dinner of restaurant caliber. On a night that I want an easy supper, I open one of these precious jars and turn a simple salmon fillet or lamb steak into a gourmet dish.

Sauces are often my key to making food exciting. The choice of cooking technique is less crucial. Am I going to broil the fish or poach it? Sear the pork or duck breast and finish it in the oven or simply broil it? It almost doesn't matter. The cooking technique I select is more often than not based on the time I have to get dinner together, rather than a burning culinary desire. If I have a bottle of wine already open, poaching the fish may be faster than roasting, as I don't have to heat the oven. If I want a crunchy surface, I may decide to broil.

What is most important to me is how the fish, duck, or pork is to be seasoned and sauced. Sometimes I don't get home in time to marinate the meat or fish long enough for an intense flavor infusion. That's when a good premade sauce is invaluable to provide maximum flavor with minimum effort. Some sauces are meant to act as condiments and are served on the side. Some can be thinned with oil and lemon juice or vinegar to make wonderful vinaigrettes for salads. Others can be heated and thinned with wine or stock to make a pan sauce to spoon over cooked food.

MOLHO di PIMENTÃO

In Brazil, this sauce, or *molho*, is a traditional accompaniment for the greens that come with the classic *feijoada*, the national dish of black beans and mixed meats, and is also spooned over dishes served at a *churrasco* (mixed grill). (The sauce is so popular that it has been adopted by Portuguese who tasted it in Brazil.) It can do double duty as an intensely flavorful quick marinade for chicken, flank or skirt steak, shrimp, or fish before broiling or grilling, or it may be drizzled on cooked fish, shellfish, simple braised greens, or into a soup for a spike of heat and acidity. A spoonful goes a long way to brighten up White Bean Guazzetto with Shellfish and Greens (page 47) or Tortilla and Lime Soup (page 39).

MAKES ½ CUP

½ cup fresh lemon juice

4 cloves garlic, finely minced

3 or 4 jalapeño chiles, seeds included, finely minced, to taste

Freshly ground black pepper

In a small bowl, whisk together the lemon juice, garlic, chiles, and lots of pepper. Store in a jar in the refrigerator for up to 2 months.

Variations: Use fresh lime juice for part of the lemon juice and/or try different chiles such as serrano or Thai. Stir the *molho* into melted butter for drizzling over cooked corn.

To extend the *molho* into a salsa, add ½ cup diced avocado and/or ¼ cup chopped tomatoes or diced mango, papaya, or peach. The salsa is good spooned on cooked fish, poultry, or pork.

ROMESCO SAUCE

This is my house "ketchup." Ever since I first tasted *romesco* sauce in Barcelona many years ago, I have been in love with its smoky, nutty richness. I would never want to be without it, as it elevates everything it touches.

A few words about *pimentón de la Vera:* It is Spanish paprika, but the peppers have been dried over a hardwood fire so the paprika has a smoky undertone. It really makes the sauce sing. You can use a mixture of sweet and hot Hungarian paprikas, but the finished *romesco* sauce will lack that smoky nuance. Look for *pimentón de la Vera* in specialty-food stores or in shops specializing in Spanish products.

Serve the sauce with boiled or grilled lobster or spread it atop a lobster while it roasts (see page 109). It also complements broiled or sautéed shrimp, sautéed scallops, or fried or broiled fish and can be smeared liberally over broiled or pan-seared lamb chops.

MAKES ABOUT 2 CUPS

2 medium-size ancho chiles or 1 rounded teaspoon ancho chile powder

1 cup almonds or hazelnuts, or a combination, toasted

4 large cloves garlic, minced

1 large red bell pepper, roasted, peeled, seeded, and chopped

1 cup peeled, seeded, and diced tomatoes (fresh or canned) or 2 tablespoons tomato paste

1 tablespoon sweet *pimentón* or sweet paprika

1/2 teaspoon hot *pimentón* or cayenne pepper, or to taste

3 tablespoons red wine vinegar

1 teaspoon salt

3/4 cup extra-virgin olive oil, preferably Spanish

If using whole anchos, soak the chiles in hot water to cover for about 1 hour. Drain, remove the stems and seeds, and cut up into small pieces. Transfer the chile pieces, or ancho chile powder, if using, to a food processor along with the nuts, garlic, roasted pepper, tomatoes, the sweet and hot *pimentón*, vinegar, and salt. Pulse a few times to make a chunky paste. Now start adding the oil a bit at a time until the mixture emulsifies. Taste. Let the sauce rest for about 15 minutes for the flavors to come together, taste again, and then decide if you want it spicier, saltier, or more vinegary, and adjust accordingly. The sauce keeps, tightly capped, in the refrigerator for up to 6 months. If the oil has risen to the top, you may want to re-emulsify it in the food processor or you can remix it back to a smooth consistency with a small whisk.

Romesco Mayonnaise: In a small bowl, whisk together about ¼ cup mayonnaise and ½ cup *romesco*. Adjust the seasoning, as you may want more salt or a bit more acidity. Add the mayonnaise to a fish soup as you might add a dollop of *rouille* or aioli, or serve it as a dip for fried potatoes, grilled or steamed asparagus, green beans, cooked beets, artichokes, or hard-boiled eggs. It also can be a spread for sandwiches or tossed with cooked chicken or shrimp for a salad. The mayonnaise keeps for about 3 weeks in the refrigerator.

Romesco Vinaigrette: Thin ½ cup *romesco* with ¼ cup olive oil and 2 tablespoons red wine vinegar or sherry vinegar. Serve over salad greens and chunks of tuna or shellfish, hard-boiled eggs, green beans, and potatoes. The vinaigrette will keep for a week in the refrigerator.

PEPPERY PRUNE SAUCE

MAKES ABOUT 2 CUPS

12 ounces pitted prunes (also called dried plums), quartered

2 cups orange juice

2 tablespoons grated orange zest

3 tablespoons honey

Pinch of ground cloves or cinnamon

1 teaspoon freshly ground black pepper, or to taste

¼ cup fresh lemon juice

While I was doing research for *Enoteca: Simple, Delicious Recipes in the Italian Wine Tradition,* I came across the idea for this sauce. I didn't have a recipe, just a brief description of a prune condiment to serve as an accompaniment for cheese. So after creating a recipe and testing it, I put the remaining sauce in a jar in the refrigerator. One night I came home with a piece of salmon, and I opened a bottle of Pinot Noir. I spotted the jar of prune condiment and I like salmon with fresh plum and fresh rhubarb sauces, so I quickly decided that the peppery prune ought to work well with the salmon, too. I have since found multiple uses for this sweet-and-tart sauce. It's great with roast pork tenderloin or broiled lamb chops, warmed slightly or at room temperature, served on the side for dipping, like chutney. Or I thin it with water, wine, or stock and use it as a basting sauce. I can poach a fillet of salmon in a light red wine and thin the sauce with some red wine, heat it through, and spoon it over the poached fish. Or I sauté a duck breast (see page 134) and add the prune sauce along with some poultry stock for a pan sauce to spoon over the cooked duck.

In a saucepan, combine the prunes, orange juice and zest, honey, and cloves over low heat and simmer, stirring from time to time, until the prunes break down to form a saucelike consistency, about 20 minutes. Stir in the pepper and lemon juice and simmer for 2 minutes. Now taste for balance. Need more lemon? More honey? More spice? If it's too thick, add water to thin to a spoonable consistency. Just simmer for a few minutes longer to meld the tastes after making adjustments. Store in a jar in the refrigerator for up to 4 months.

Sautéed Duck Breast (page 134) with Peppery Prune Sauce

POMEGRANATE MARINADE and BASTING SAUCE

MAKES ABOUT 1²/₃ CUPS

¹/₃ cup pomegranate molasses, preferably Cortas brand

¹/₂ cup honey, heated until liquified

¹/₂ cup dry red wine

1 tablespoon freshly ground black pepper

¹/₄ cup pure olive oil

I love the sweet-tart taste of pomegranate syrup and its thicker version, pomegranate molasses. (They can be found in stores specializing in imported foods from the Middle East.) By combining pomegranate molasses with wine, honey, and some olive oil, I have a wonderful marinade for roasted or broiled pork, broiled lamb chops or chicken pieces, or kabobs. Use just enough to coat the meat or poultry, leaving it to marinate for 1 to 3 hours, then brush with a bit more during cooking. It caramelizes beautifully over the meat, providing crunch and a sweet, smoky char. The pomegranate mixture also can be used as a basting sauce if you haven't had time to marinate the meat.

In a bowl, whisk together the pomegranate molasses, honey, and wine. Whisk in the pepper and olive oil. Store in a jar in the refrigerator for up to 3 months.

PEANUT SAUCE

This popular Southeast Asian sauce is excellent with grilled chicken, flank steak, lamb chops, pork loin, or even fish and shellfish. It makes a great dipping sauce for all manner of kabobs.

MAKES ABOUT 2 1/2 CUPS

1 cup unsalted smooth peanut butter

1/3 cup finely chopped dry-roasted peanuts

1 tablespoon sugar

2 tablespoons fresh lemon juice

1/2 cup canned sweetened coconut cream, such as Coco Lopez brand

1/3 cup soy sauce

2/3 cup chicken stock or water

1/2 teaspoon finely minced garlic

1 teaspoon red pepper flakes, or to taste

1 teaspoon ground cumin

1 teaspoon ground coriander

In a small saucepan, combine all of the ingredients and bring to a boil over medium heat, stirring often. Simmer, stirring occasionally, for 2 minutes to combine well.

To serve, reheat gently, whisking in a bit of water as needed for a spoonable consistency. Store in a jar in the refrigerator. It will keep for up to 4 months.

Note: If you use canned coconut milk rather than cream, you may want to add a bit more sugar.

MANGO CHUTNEY

I find that most commercial chutneys are too dry and the texture of the fruit is often tough, so I like to make my own. Chutney will keep for a very long time. If you are nervous about putting it up in canning jars for shelf storage, you can make a batch and store it in the refrigerator for up to a year. This chutney is good with curried food and fried chicken, and it also will give roast chicken, turkey, and pork tenderloin or chops a lift.

To test preserves for doneness, I keep a small stack of little plates in the freezer. I drop some of the chutney or jam on a cold plate, and if it sets up within a matter of minutes, rather than run all over the place, it is ready.

MAKES ABOUT 4 CUPS

1 small onion, diced

1 clove garlic

1 juicy lime, cut into small pieces

2 ounces fresh ginger, peeled and thinly sliced across the grain

1 cup cider vinegar

½ cup peeled, diced mangoes (2 to 3 mangoes)

1 cup firmly packed brown sugar

½ teaspoon salt

1 teaspoon ground cinnamon

¼ teaspoon ground allspice

¼ teaspoon ground cloves

¼ teaspoon cayenne pepper, or to taste

½ cup dark or golden raisins

In a blender or food processor, combine the onion, garlic, lime, ginger, and ½ cup of the vinegar and process to a purée.

Put the mangoes in a preserving kettle or a deep, heavy nonreactive pot. (I prefer enameled cast iron or anodized aluminum.) Add the onion-ginger purée, sugar, spices, and the remaining ½ cup vinegar. Stir well to combine. Bring to a boil over medium heat, stirring occasionally. Simmer until thick, stirring from time to time; it should take about 30 minutes. Add the raisins during the last 10 minutes of cooking and stir often to prevent scorching. (Raisins tend to sink to the bottom.) To test if the chutney is ready, use the cold-plate test (see recipe introduction). Alternatively, use a candy thermometer; it should register 210° to 215°F.

Spoon into sterilized canning jars, seal, and process for 10 to 15 minutes in a boiling-water bath, then store in a cool, dark cupboard for up to 2 years. Or spoon into clean jars or plastic containers with tight-fitting lids and keep in the refrigerator.

RUSSIAN HOT-and-SWEET MUSTARD

When I was growing up in Brooklyn, my mother used to buy mustard like this one from one of our neighborhood delicatessens. It was an essential accompaniment to cold boiled tongue or brisket. I also love it with roasted pork tenderloin and find it a fine alternative to Chinese hot mustard. A spoonful or two makes a wonderful addition to a sauce or vinaigrette and will enliven even the stodgiest sandwich. If it should separate or settle a bit while stored, just stir before using. Although I have given instructions for a hand method, the mustard can be made in a food processor or electric mixer as well.

MAKES ABOUT 1½ CUPS

4 ounces Colman's dry mustard powder

¼ cup distilled white vinegar

4 tablespoons water

¼ cup sugar

1 tablespoon salt

1 egg

1 cup pure olive oil or canola oil

In a bowl, whisk together the mustard, vinegar, 2 tablespoons of the water, the sugar, and salt. (You can stabilize the bowl by putting a damp towel underneath it so it doesn't wobble as you whisk.) Beat in the egg, then start to add the oil drop by drop, as if making a mayonnaise, while whisking constantly. Adjust the seasoning (sugar, salt, vinegar) and thin with the remaining 2 tablespoons water. Store in a covered jar or other container in the refrigerator for up to 3 months.

SUN GOLD TOMATO CHUTNEY

Tomato chutney can be made with green, yellow, or red cherry or plum-shaped tomatoes. The red and yellow look attractive over time, but the green tomatoes darken considerably. I serve this chutney with lamb chops, roast or fried chicken, curries, and even pair it with creamy goat or sheep's cheese.

MAKES ABOUT 5 CUPS

1 onion, chopped

4 cloves garlic

6 ounces fresh ginger, peeled and thinly sliced across the grain

2 jalapeño chiles

½ cup cider vinegar

½ teaspoon cayenne pepper, or to taste

½ teaspoon ground cinnamon

2 teaspoons salt, or to taste

1 tablespoon garam masala or curry powder

4 cups Sun Gold cherry tomatoes (about 2 pounds), stems removed, washed

1 cup sugar

1 juicy lemon, sliced paper-thin and then cut into smallish pieces

In a blender or food processor, combine the onion, garlic, ginger, chiles, and vinegar and grind to a paste. Add the spices and pulse to combine. Put the tomatoes in a preserving kettle or a deep, heavy nonreactive pot. Add the onion mixture, sugar, and lemon pieces to the pot. Gradually bring to a boil over medium heat, stirring occasionally. Simmer until thick, stirring from time to time; it should take about 30 to 45 minutes. If the mixture seems dry, add a bit more vinegar or water. To test if it is ready, use the cold-plate test (see recipe introduction, page 28), or use a candy thermometer; it should register 210 to 215°F. Spoon into sterilized canning jars, seal, and process for 10 to 15 minutes in a boiling-water bath, then store in a cool, dark cupboard for up to 2 years. Or spoon into clean jars or plastic containers with tight-fitting lids and keep in the refrigerator for up to 1 year.

INDONESIAN SWEET SOY SAUCE

Asian sauces are an invaluable addition to the pantry. This is an excellent marinade for fish, shellfish, pork, beef, and poultry. It also can be spooned over the meat or seafood after cooking. You can vary its flavor by adding grated fresh ginger or hot pepper. Indonesian Sweet Soy Sauce keeps in the refrigerator for up to 1 month.

MAKES 1½ CUPS

1 cup soy sauce

½ cup firmly packed brown sugar

¼ cup fresh lemon juice

2 tablespoons peeled and grated fresh ginger (optional)

1 tablespoon minced garlic (optional)

1 teaspoon red pepper flakes, or to taste (optional)

In a saucepan, combine the soy sauce, sugar, lemon juice, and 1 or more of the optional ingredients, if desired. Bring to a simmer over medium heat and cook for 5 minutes to blend the flavors. Store in a tightly capped jar. If you have not added the optimal ingredients during the initial preparation, you can simply reheat the sauce, add 1 or more of the ingredients, and simmer for a few minutes to blend the flavors.

Note: For mouth-feel and extra smoothness, enrich the sauce with melted butter or coconut milk. I add them as I use the sauce. This whole batch can support ½ cup (1 stick) unsalted butter, melted, or up to 2 cups canned coconut milk. Use warm as a finishing sauce on cooked fish, shellfish, poultry, and pork.

PESTO

Pesto is almost the perfect condiment. It can be made weeks ahead of time and kept in the refrigerator or may be frozen. It's good on pasta, spooned into soup or over cooked vegetables, or served as a sauce for cooked fish. Moderation is important, however. When it is good, it is hard to resist.

Fresh basil varies in flavor from week to week and from batch to batch. Sometimes, ironically enough, hothouse basil is sweeter than field basil. In very hot weather, basil grown outdoors can become bitter and metallic tasting. Taste a leaf before you buy. Smaller leaves are milder in flavor; they are also softer and thus easier to mash or purée.

MAKES ABOUT 1½ CUPS

2 cups tightly packed fresh basil leaves

2 teaspoons finely chopped garlic

2 tablespoons pine nuts or walnuts, toasted

1 teaspoon salt

½ teaspoon freshly ground black pepper

½ to ¾ cup pure olive oil

¼ cup grated Parmesan cheese (optional)

In a blender or food processor, combine the basil, garlic, nuts, salt, and pepper. Add about half of the olive oil and process briefly to mix. With the motor running, gradually add the rest of the olive oil, using only as much as you need to form a thick purée. Do not overblend or overprocess. You should be able to see tiny pieces of basil leaf rather than a homogenous green paste. If the pesto is to be used exclusively for pasta, add the Parmesan cheese. Also, if you are using the cheese, hold back on the salt until after adding the cheese. You may find that you will not need as much, as Parmesan is rather salty.

Transfer the pesto to a jar and pour a little olive oil on top to maintain its bright green color. Pesto will keep for many weeks in the refrigerator. It may be frozen, but preferably without the cheese and garlic. You might be better off just chopping the basil with the oil in the blender or processor and freezing that mixture instead, and then adding the other ingredients when it comes time to use it.

Pesto Vinaigrette: Whisk together ¼ cup pesto with ¼ cup extra-virgin or pure olive oil and 2 tablespoons white wine vinegar.

AIOLI

This garlic-scented mayonnaise is the basis for many other sauces. By itself, aioli may be used as a dip for cooked asparagus, artichokes, beets, potatoes, and green beans; as a sandwich spread; mixed with chopped egg yolks for filling deviled eggs; or added as a generous dollop to enhance a fish soup or stew.

MAKES ABOUT 1 CUP

1 egg yolk

2 tablespoons fresh lemon juice

3/4 to 1 cup pure olive oil

1 tablespoon finely minced garlic, ground to a fine paste with 1 teaspoon kosher or coarse sea salt with a mortar and pestle

Place the egg yolk in a blender or food processor. Add a bit of the lemon juice and process briefly. Then, with the motor running, add the olive oil, a few drops at a time, until a thick emulsion is formed. The oil may be added more quickly once the mixture emulsifies. Add the remaining lemon juice and then the garlic to taste. If the aioli is too thick, thin with a little water.

Of course you may instead make the aioli in a bowl with a whisk. It is a satisfying experience, and the texture of the mayonnaise is a little lighter than if you assemble it in a processor or blender. Put a damp towel under the bowl to stabilize it so you don't have to hold it. Whisk together the egg yolk and a little lemon juice, and then add the oil, drop by drop, with one hand while whisking madly with the other.

Rouille: Add a bit of tomato paste for color and hot *pimentón* (see Romesco Sauce, page 22) to taste.

Red Pepper Aioli: Fold in 1 small red bell pepper, roasted, peeled, seeded, and puréed, and a bit of lemon juice.

Caesar Salad Dressing: Combine half of the aioli with 3/4 teaspoon minced anchovy fillets, 1 1/2 teaspoons Dijon mustard, 1/4 teaspoon Worcestershire sauce, 1 1/2 tablespoons grated Parmesan cheese, and lots of freshly ground black pepper in the blender or food processor and process to emulsify. This makes enough for 1 large dinner salad.

Ginger Aioli: Add up to 1 tablespoon peeled and finely grated fresh ginger to the aioli.

Chinese Chicken Salad Dressing: Add 2 tablespoons peeled and finely grated fresh ginger, 1 tablespoon hot-and-sweet mustard (page 29 or store-bought), 1 tablespoon soy sauce, 1 tablespoon white vinegar, and 1 1/2 teaspoons sesame oil to the aioli. Use to dress a salad of romaine, bean sprouts, slivers of cucumber, and strips of cooked chicken. It is also good spooned on cooked tuna, hot or cold, or on cooked artichokes or asparagus. This makes enough for 2 large dinner salads.

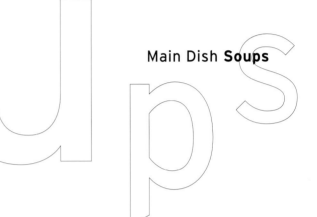

Main Dish **Soups**

Main Dish **Soups**

If I eat a bowl of soup as a first course, I find that I'm often too full to finish the main course. When I cook for myself at home, however, I don't usually make a series of courses, so a big bowl of soup can be my entire meal—the perfect solo supper. I start with a simple base and keep adding relevant ingredients until I have a stewy, filling soup.

In the winter, legumes, grains, and pasta are the means to achieving a comforting and satisfying soup meal. Leftover bread or tortillas also add body to extend a stock base. Soup is an ideal vehicle for using leftover meat or poultry, bits of cooked greens, or other vegetables, too. Shellfish, which always seem to add a touch of luxury to a meal, can turn a staid soup into a special-occasion repast.

Soup is a good candidate for reheating, so it pays to make two portions of the basic recipe. You can always play with additions with subsequent reheats.

TORTILLA and LIME SOUP

On a vacation in the Yucatán in Mexico, I tasted my first bowl of *sopa di lima*. In its pure, stripped-down form, it was a delightful first course that awakened my appetite. Over the years, I have played with the basic recipe and have added diced avocado, corn, and even rice to make the soup substantial enough to be supper. *Sopa di lima* is usually made with chicken, but I find that shrimp works well, too. My one caveat about this soup is to be careful not to "overheat" the stock with excessive chiles. The first bite may be fine, but heat increases with every mouthful, possibly making the soup too fiery for comfort. What is important is the balance between the tartness of the lime and the heat of the chiles.

If using raw chicken, poach the chicken breast in a saucepan with stock to cover until just cooked through, about 8 minutes. You may poach the breast whole and then shred the meat, or you may cut the breast into ½-inch-wide pieces and poach them. They will cook in half the time. If using cooked chicken or turkey, cut into ½ inch-wide strips. You should have about 1 cup. If using raw shrimp, simmer them in stock to cover for 2 minutes. You can instead cook them in their shells in the stock used for the soup ahead of time, to give the soup a more shrimpy taste, then peel and devein them, or you may add them, already peeled and deveined, during the last 2 minutes of cooking the soup.

continued

6 ounces boneless, skinless raw chicken breast, leftover cooked chicken or turkey, or raw small or medium shrimp, peeled and deveined

Chicken stock or water for poaching the chicken, if needed, plus 4 cups chicken stock reduced to 2 cups

1 tablespoon olive oil

⅓ cup diced onion

1 teaspoon minced garlic

½ teaspoon finely minced jalapeño chile, or to taste

½ cup peeled, seeded, and diced tomatoes (fresh or canned)

Kernels from 1 ear of corn (about ¾ cup)

2 tablespoons minced green onion, including tender green tops

1 tablespoon chopped fresh cilantro

1 to 2 tablespoons fresh lime juice, to taste

½ teaspoon salt, or to taste

¼ teaspoon freshly ground black pepper

Canola or corn oil for frying tortillas

1 or 2 corn tortillas, cut into strips 1 ½ inches long and ½ inch wide

½ avocado, peeled, pitted, and diced

2 paper-thin lime slices, each quartered

To make the soup base, in a saucepan, heat the olive oil over medium heat. Add the onion and sauté until translucent, about 8 minutes. Add the garlic and chile and sauté, stirring, for 1 to 2 minutes. Add the reduced stock and bring to a boil. Add the tomatoes, corn, green onion, cilantro, lime juice, salt, and pepper. Simmer for 2 minutes to blend the flavors. If you are using shrimp and haven't cooked them, add them now; if you are using leftover cooked chicken, add it now as well. Cook for 2 minutes. Taste and adjust seasoning.

While the soup simmers, pour the canola oil to the depth of about 1 inch in a small, deep sauté pan and heat over medium heat. When the oil is hot, add the tortilla strips and fry briefly until golden and crisp. Drain on paper towels.

Put the avocado in a large bowl and pour the hot soup over it. Top with the pieces of lime and the tortilla strips.

Variation: For a version that is less soupy and more like *chilaquiles,* use only 3/4 cup stock and add 2 torn tortillas to the mixture to heat through. Omit the fried tortilla strips and top with 1/3 cup shredded Monterey Jack cheese.

CHICKEN and BREAD SOUP

4 tablespoons (½ stick) unsalted butter

1 tablespoon olive oil

½ onion, cut into small dice

1 celery stalk, cut into small dice

1 small carrot, peeled and cut into small dice

2 boneless, skinless chicken thighs (5 to 8 ounces total weight), trimmed and cut into 1-inch pieces or 1 generous cup cubed (1 inch) cooked chicken or turkey

¼ cup dry white wine

2 cups chicken stock

Salt and freshly ground black pepper

Pinch of ground cinnamon

¼ cup cooked sliced mushrooms (optional)

½ cup diced cooked butternut squash (optional)

2 slices country-style bread, ½ inch thick, crusts removed, or 1 thick slice bread

¼ cup grated Parmesan cheese, preferably Parmigiano Reggiano, or part Fontina and part Parmigiano Reggiano

This recipe is a cross between a *panada,* or bread soup, and a classic Venetian dish called *sopa coada. Panada* takes its name from *pane,* which means "bread," because bread is a central ingredient in the soup. Some versions call for soaking the bread in liquid, then whisking the crumbs into the stock for a thick purée. Others bake the bread in layers with the stock for a thickened, cakey soup you carve out with a spoon. *Sopa coada,* a dialect name, comes from the Italian verb *covare,* which means "to brood," "to hatch," or "to smolder." More like a poultry bread pudding than a soup, it is rich and filling, so it is ideal for a solo supper. Traditionally, layers of sautéed country bread are topped with boned, braised pigeon (squab), aromatic vegetables, and grated Parmesan cheese, then covered with a rich pigeon stock and baked for many hours. The aromatic dish emerges golden, the stock fully absorbed, the bread soft and pudding-like. While I love squab, I usually make this soup with chicken, especially with my habit of making roast chicken with guaranteed leftovers. You can make this soup even richer and more filling by adding mushrooms or butternut squash.

In a wide saucepan, melt 2 tablespoons of the butter with the olive oil over medium heat. When the mixture is bubbling, add the diced vegetables and sauté until softened, about 10 minutes. If using raw chicken, add it now and sauté, turning occasionally, until golden, about 5 minutes. Add the wine and cook until it evaporates. Then add the chicken stock, salt and pepper to taste, and the cinnamon and cover the pan. Simmer gently, until the chicken is tender, 20 to 30 minutes. If using cooked chicken, mushrooms, and squash, add during the last 10 minutes of cooking.

Comfort Food

When you have a bad day, certain foods can help ease the pain. For many people, fancy food isn't the cure. It seems too self-conscious and requires too much thinking and attention. On the other hand, comfort food requires no thought or effort to eat it. That's why it works. Comfort food promotes well-being and peace of mind. It is generally a familiar food, often with happy memories attached to it. It might be a pint of peach ice cream or a fudgy brownie. For me it's usually a big soup; a bowl of risotto, *farro,* or soft polenta with cheese; a grilled cheese sandwich; or softly scrambled eggs with toast—all dishes to eat with a spoon or fingers, curled up on the couch, with book in hand. Time heals. Food comforts.

Meanwhile, melt the remaining 2 tablespoons butter in a large sauté pan over medium heat. Add the bread and sauté, turning once, until pale gold on both sides. (Or toast it and spread lightly with the butter while warm.)

You now have two options. The first is fast and easy: Cut the bread into croutons and place them in a big soup bowl. Pour the hot chicken and vegetable soup over the croutons and then top with the cheese. You may brown it under the broiler, first making sure the bowl is flameproof.

If you are not in a hurry and want to replicate the *coada* style, option two is the better choice: Preheat the oven to 300°F. Place a slice of the bread in a deep ovenproof bowl, such as a potpie dish or onion-soup crock. Sprinkle some of the cheese on top, and then the chicken and vegetables. Top with the other slice of bread. (It can be assembled up to this point 8 hours ahead of time and refrigerated until you are ready to bake it.) Ladle the stock over the top and sprinkle with the remaining cheese. Cover loosely with aluminum foil. Put the bowl on a baking sheet, as it may bubble over, and bake for 30 to 60 minutes, depending on the depth of the soup. The bread on the bottom should be custardy, and the bread on the top should be chewy. If you want a crusty top, do not cover with foil. For added crunch, slip it under the broiler to brown.

LENTIL and FARRO SOUP

1/4 cup *farro*

1 tablespoon olive oil

3 tablespoons diced pancetta

1/2 onion, diced

1 small carrot, peeled and diced

1 small celery stalk, diced

1 teaspoon chopped fresh thyme, sage, or marjoram

Salt

Pinch of ground cinnamon (optional)

1/3 cup green lentils, French or Italian, picked over and rinsed

1/2 bay leaf

2 cups water or meat or poultry stock

1 tablespoon tomato paste

5 to 6 cooked chestnuts, coarsely crumbled into chunks (optional)

Freshly ground black pepper

2 teaspoons chopped fresh flat-leaf parsley

Extra-virgin olive oil for serving

Grated Parmesan cheese for serving

One very cold January, I was traveling in the Abruzzo region of Italy. The wind whipped through the streets of the towns, chilling me to the bone. This legume and *farro* soup was my salvation on many a day. The best version was served at a small family-run restaurant high on a mountain-top at Rocca di Calascio. The chef-owner, whose four children were doing homework in the dining room when I arrived, used four kinds of legumes—lentils, white beans, black-eyed peas, and red beans—along with *farro* and chopped pancetta. While this may sound complicated, it was simplicity itself compared to the traditional ancestor of this regional soup, the famous *le virtù,* which combines seven beans, seven vegetables, and seven cuts of meat, mostly from the pig, then *farro* or small pasta. One story says that the soup symbolizes the virtues and thriftiness of the local women who have never let anything go to waste in the kitchen. Another story says it was a test to see which virtuous woman would devote herself to such a complex dish requiring so many steps.

When I cook for friends and family, I usually make a large batch of this soup with an assortment of beans, but when I am cooking it just for me, I simplify the recipe, using only lentils, as they do not require soaking. In the winter, I love to cook up a batch of chestnuts to serve as a side dish or to use in pilafs and soups. (You can also buy them already cooked and vacuum-packed.) They add a rich sweetness that enlivens the starchy lentils. While you can cook the *farro* directly in the soup, I cook it separately, as I am fanatic about texture. For information on *farro,* see page 77. You can double this recipe and have enough for another night. A bit more stock might be needed when you reheat.

Cook the *farro* in a generous amount of salted boiling water. When the grains are soft but still have some firmness in the center, after about 20 minutes, drain and set aside.

In a saucepan, heat the olive oil over medium heat. Add the pancetta and sauté until translucent, about 5 minutes. Add the onion, carrot, celery, and thyme and cook, stirring, until tender, about 8 minutes, adding salt to taste and the cinnamon, if using. (The cinnamon will play up the sweetness of the onion, pancetta, and chestnuts.) Add the lentils, bay leaf, water, and tomato paste and bring to a boil. Reduce the heat to low, cover, and simmer until the lentils are tender but not falling apart, about 30 minutes.

Add the chestnuts, if using, and the cooked *farro* and simmer for 10 minutes to heat through and blend the flavors. Season to taste with salt and pepper. Pour into a warmed soup bowl and garnish with the chopped parsley, a drizzle of extra-virgin olive oil, and the grated cheese.

Variation: *Farro* is also a specialty of the Garfagnana region, above Lucca in Tuscany, where thinly sliced dark kale, or *cavolo nero*, as well as a few diced tomatoes, is added to the basic bean soup. Sometimes a piece of prosciutto is added along with the beans for a more meaty flavor. If you cannot find *farro* at your market, you may substitute spelt or wheat berries, both of which will take twice as long to cook. Cooked chickpeas or white beans can be added to the soup in place of some of the lentils.

WHITE BEAN GUAZZETTO with SHELLFISH and GREENS

From the Italian verb *guazzare,* which means "to splash about," this stewlike bean soup, swimming with seafood, is often called a *guazzetto.* Spanish cooks make a similar soup, sometimes substituting chickpeas for the white beans, while Portuguese cooks make the related *feijoada branca.* In other words, this is a classic Mediterranean combination.

I like to play with the garnishes. If I'm feeling nostalgic for Spain, I add a *picada* of toasted almonds and garlic. Another night I might add a spoonful of Portuguese *molho di pimentão* (page 21). Or I could stay in Italian mode by adding a dollop of pesto (page 33). I could even add cooked chopped greens to extend the soup and make a more filling meal. What I like about the *guazzetto* is the contrast of the bland creaminess of the beans alongside the sweetness of the mussels or the saltiness of clams, the slight acidity of the tomatoes, and the bitterness of the greens. Sometimes I am extravagant and add shrimp or lobster. Chunks of a firm, meaty fish such as cod or halibut could be used as well. If the soup isn't filling enough, serve with grilled bread. If you tend to plan ahead, make a double batch of white beans to have on hand for another soup or salad.

1/3 cup dried white beans

1/2 onion, plus 1/2 cup chopped onion

1 clove garlic, peeled but left whole, plus 1 teaspoon finely minced garlic

1/2 bay leaf

1 teaspoon salt

1 tablespoon olive oil

Pinch of red pepper flakes (optional)

1/2 cup peeled, seeded, and diced tomatoes (fresh or canned)

1 pound mussels or clams, well scrubbed and mussels debearded, or 6 ounces shrimp or lobster meat

1/4 cup dry white wine

A large handful of spinach, chard, or escarole, cut into fine strips

Pick over the dried beans and remove any stones or debris. Rinse well, put in a saucepan, and cover with 2 cups cold water. Bring to a boil, reduce the heat to medium and cook for 2 minutes. Remove from the heat and let stand for 1 hour. Drain the beans and return them to the saucepan with fresh water to cover by about 2 inches. Add the 1/2 onion, the whole garlic clove, and the bay leaf and bring to a boil over medium-high heat. Reduce the heat to low, add the salt, cover, and simmer until beans are tender but not falling apart, about 40 minutes. Remove and discard the onion, garlic, and bay and set the beans aside with their liquid.

continued

In a saucepan, heat the olive oil over medium heat. Add the chopped onion and cook, stirring, until tender, 8 to 10 minutes. Add the minced garlic and the red pepper flakes, if using, and cook for a minute longer. Add the tomatoes and the white beans and their liquid and simmer for 2 minutes. Remove from the heat and set aside.

In a large sauté pan, combine the mussels and the wine. Bring to a boil, cover, and steam until the shellfish open. Transfer the shellfish to a bowl, discarding any that fail to open. Strain the pan juices through a cheesecloth-lined sieve held over a bowl and add to the beans. Remove the meat from the shells and discard the shells.

Reheat the beans, then add the greens and let them wilt. Then add the mussels. If using shrimp or lobster, add now and heat through. Taste and adjust the seasoning. Thin with water if needed. Garnish as suggested in the introduction.

Variation: You can add ½ cup cooked short pasta to this soup during the last few minutes of cooking for a seafood *pasta e fagioli*.

ASIAN-STYLE NOODLE SOUP

This soup can be as opulent as you like. Instead of seafood, you can use cooked chicken, a combination of chicken and shrimp, or just vegetables. Snow peas, mung bean sprouts, mushrooms, and spinach are all at your disposal for a more filling or less filling meal. The amount of stock you need is determined by how many noodles you add to the soup.

6 ounces shrimp in the shell or crabmeat

6 ounces fresh Chinese egg noodles

1 clove garlic

1 shallot, cut up

2 green onions, cut up

1/2 stalk lemongrass, tender purple tinged part only, cut up

1 tablespoon peeled and thinly sliced fresh ginger

1/2 jalapeño chile, chopped

1 tablespoon canola oil

2 cups chicken, shrimp (see Note), or other complementary stock

1 teaspoon grated lime zest

4 mushrooms, wiped clean and thinly sliced

4 to 6 snow peas, cut on the diagonal into 1/2-inch-wide strips

1/2 cup mung bean sprouts or 1 cup shredded spinach or watercress leaves

1 tablespoon fresh lime juice

Salt and freshly ground black pepper

2 teaspoons finely slivered fresh basil

2 teaspoons finely slivered fresh mint

Peel and devein the shrimp. If they are large, cut them in half lengthwise or into bite-size pieces. If using crabmeat, pick over for any shell fragments.

Parboil the noodles in boiling salted water for a minute or two, then drain and set aside.

In a food processor or blender, combine the garlic, shallots, green onions, lemongrass, ginger, and chile and pulse until a paste forms.

In a saucepan, heat the oil over medium heat. Add the paste and cook for 5 minutes, stirring often. Add the stock and lime zest and simmer for 5 minutes. Add the noodles, shrimp, mushrooms, snow peas, and sprouts and simmer until the shrimp turn pink, about 3 minutes.

Season the soup with lime juice and salt and pepper to taste. Add the basil and mint and pour into a warmed soup bowl.

Note: If you have used shrimp, you can make a wonderful fragrant stock with the shrimp shells. Sauté the shells in a tablespoon or two of canola oil until they turn pink, then add the lemongrass trimmings, a couple of ginger slices, a small dried chile, and water to cover. Bring to a boil and simmer 20 minutes, then strain through a cheesecloth-lined sieve.

PERSIAN MEATBALL SOUP

When I am in the mood to cook, I enjoy preparing meatballs as a mildly meditative activity. I usually make a double
batch, use some for a pan sauté, and save some for a soup
supper or maybe for pasta. Certainly the *guazzetto* of white
beans with greens (page 47) would welcome meatballs
instead of seafood. My favorite meatball soup, however, is
Persian. It has a yogurt base bound with egg and flour and
must not boil, or the yogurt will curdle. The turmeric tints
the soup a lovely pale yellow, which is set off by the green
of the mint and green onions and the brown of the meatballs. When pomegranates are in season, I sprinkle a few of
the jewel-like red seeds on top.

¼ cup dried chickpeas

½ teaspoon salt, plus more to taste

¼ cup dried green or black lentils

6 ounces ground beef

3 tablespoons grated yellow onion

1 egg, lightly beaten and then divided in 2 equal portions

¼ teaspoon freshly ground black pepper, plus more to taste

½ teaspoon ground cinnamon

½ cup low-fat plain yogurt

1 teaspoon all-purpose flour

¼ teaspoon ground turmeric

2 tablespoons basmati rice

2 to 3 cups chicken stock or water

2 tablespoons chopped fresh flat-leaf parsley

2 tablespoons chopped green onion, including tender green tops

2 tablespoons chopped fresh mint

1 tablespoon unsalted butter

1 clove garlic, very finely minced

Pomegranate seeds (optional)

Pick over the dried chickpeas and remove any stones
or debris. Rinse well, put in a saucepan, and cover with 1 cup
cold water. Bring to a boil, reduce the heat to medium, and
cook for 2 minutes. Remove from the heat and let stand for
1 hour. Drain the beans and return them to the saucepan with
cold water to cover by about 2 inches. Bring to a boil over
medium-high heat. Reduce the heat to low, add ¼ teaspoon
of the salt, cover, and simmer until the beans are tender but
not falling apart, 40 to 50 minutes. Drain and reserve.

Pick over the lentils and remove any stones or debris.
Rinse well, put in a small saucepan, and cover with cold water.
Bring to a boil, reduce the heat to low, and simmer until
firm-tender, about 25 minutes. Drain and reserve.

In a bowl, combine the ground beef, grated onion, half of the egg, the remaining ¼ teaspoon salt, pepper, and ¼ teaspoon of the cinnamon. Mix well with your hands. Fry a tiny patty of the mixture to see if it is seasoned to your taste. Adjust the seasoning, if necessary, then form the beef mixture into tiny meatballs about the size of a nickel, or smaller if you have the patience. Refrigerate.

To make the soup base, spoon the yogurt into a medium saucepan. Whisk in the remaining half egg, the flour, turmeric, and remaining ¼ teaspoon cinnamon. Add the rice, reserved lentils and 2 cups of the stock. Place over low heat and cook gently, stirring occasionally, for about 10 minutes. Add the reserved chickpeas, parsley, green onion, and most of the chopped mint. Simmer for 10 minutes more, then add the meatballs and simmer for 10 minutes longer. Add the remaining stock if needed.

In a small sauté pan, melt the butter. Add the garlic and sauté until soft but not colored, about 2 minutes. Add to the soup and adjust the seasoning with salt and pepper. Pour into a warmed soup bowl and sprinkle with remaining mint and the pomegranate seeds, if using.

Note: You can double the meat mixture and cook the remaining half of the seasoned meat mixture as a panfried burger, top it with yogurt seasoned with garlic, and serve it in a pita bread. Or you can form the rest of the meat mixture into meatballs, sauté them in butter or oil until browned, simmer them in tomato sauce, and then serve over rice with a drizzle of garlicky yogurt.

CREAM of POTATO SOUP
with VARIATIONS

1 ½ tablespoons unsalted butter

½ cup chopped onion

1 ½ cups peeled, diced russet potatoes

2 cups chicken stock

¼ cup heavy cream, milk, or chicken stock

1 teaspoon salt, plus more to taste

½ teaspoon freshly ground black pepper

Potato soup is bland and comforting and can be a home base for endless variations and garnishes. The potatoes may be cooked with a head of garlic, or the pulp from a head of roasted garlic can be whisked into the finished soup. A swirl of tapenade or pesto and chunks of fish will take it in one direction. Croutons with melted Cheddar cheese or goat cheese add extra richness. Simply put, this soup is a blank slate awaiting an artist's signature. Select from among the variations before you begin making the soup.

In a heavy saucepan, melt the butter over medium heat. Add the onion and sauté until tender and translucent, 8 to 10 minutes. Add the potatoes and stock and bring to a boil. Reduce the heat to low and simmer, uncovered, until the potatoes are tender, 15 to 20 minutes.

Remove from the heat and add the potatoes, onion, and a little of the stock to a blender. Purée until smooth. Return the purée to the pan holding the remaining liquid and reheat gently. The soup will be thick. Thin it with the cream, season with the salt and pepper, then pour into a warmed soup bowl.

A World of Chicken Soup

As a bona fide Jewish mother, I firmly believe that nothing is more comforting than a bowl of chicken soup. However, I'm enough of a realist to know that not everyone will take the time to make chicken stock, even though it's easy to prepare. Because I believe in a well-stocked pantry, I always have some in the freezer. But for ease, low-sodium canned broth can be reduced and enriched to taste pretty good.

How you embellish chicken soup usually depends on what you may have in the refrigerator or pantry. Rice or noodles bring body to the soup. If I have time I might even make matzo balls. Of course, vegetables and pieces of chicken are great additions, too. Then there is the matter of flavor accent. Ginger and lemongrass for an Asian taste? Egg and lemon or crumbled feta for a Greek flavor palate? Grated Parmesan and eggs for a Roman *stracciatella?* I can travel the world on chicken soup.

In restaurants, the elements of a dish are often prepared separately, then combined at the last minute. I found that this technique was one of the best ways to increase my control over the quality of the end product served to our guests. Home cooking is different. There are fewer distractions and not too many orders coming in at once, just your own. You can cook the vegetables directly in the soup, and sometimes the noodles, too, and usually not risk overcooking. But for greater control and foolproof results, it's best to cook all of the components separately, reducing the margin for error. Aesthetics also come into play. Do you like the look of chicken in strips and carrots in strips, or do you like the carrots and chicken to be in uniform dice? Make a choice and be consistent. Just remember that smaller pieces cook very quickly; don't let them get too soft, as they will be reheated later in the soup.

Variations: Purée the hot soup with 1 cup chopped watercress or ½ cup chopped sorrel. The heat of the soup will set the color of the sorrel so that it remains green, rather than turn a sad gray-brown. But you have to eat it right away because reheating will dull the color.

Add some cooked fish when you reheat the puréed soup and then finish with a dollop of Pesto (page 33).

Add ½ cup chopped arugula and a little diced prosciutto when you reheat the puréed soup. Garnish with diced tomatoes and some chopped fresh basil or marjoram or a spoonful of Pesto (page 33).

Top with crumbled Gorgonzola cheese and a few fennel sprigs; with crumbled fresh goat cheese, chopped walnuts, and chopped fresh basil; with croutons topped with grated Cheddar cheese; or with croutons topped with crumbled fresh goat cheese and thyme.

Garnish with chopped fresh mint, cooked green beans, and strips of sun-dried tomatoes.

Garnish with a nice spoonful of caviar, a dollop of sour cream, and minced fresh chives.

Main Dish **Salads**

Main Dish **Salads**

If I lived in a more tropical climate, main dish salads would be an integral part of my dining routine. I love salads, but most of the time I eat them as a palate awakener or starter course, or after the main course as a palate cleanser. While I don't have a serious sweet tooth, I do have a weakness for tartness and acidity. Vinaigrettes are my passion, and creating the perfect vinaigrette for the selected assemblage of greens and garnishes is always a delightful culinary challenge. However, I rarely make a meal out of a leafy salad unless it can be made more filling with the addition of protein in the form of legumes, seafood, meat, or poultry. My other main dish salads are typically based on a grain such as rice or *farro* or on bread.

Composed salads are really room-temperature main dish suppers. They are an ideal way to use quality leftovers like cooked artichokes, asparagus, green beans, white beans, or chickpeas; boiled potatoes; and slices of cooked chicken, turkey, steak, pork, tuna, or salmon—in other words, foods that taste equally good hot or at room temperature. Here is where having a roster of vinaigrettes at your disposal can elevate simple leftovers to a fine supper. Some items in the pantry (see pages 10 to 15), such as *romesco* or pesto, thinned with oil and vinegar, make a great dressing, as do thinned aioli and other mayonnaise-based dressings. So when you are contemplating an assortment of leftovers, turn to the sauce chapter and you'll find inspiration and dressings there.

FARRO SALAD

Grain salads are ideal candidates for supper, as they are filling and provide a neutral base for other more assertive ingredients. Grown today in western Tuscany and the Abruzzo, *farro* is an ancient wheat, milder and lighter than wheat berries and more interesting than barley, to which it bears some slight affinity in appearance, texture, and subtle sweetness. Once cooked, *farro* keeps well in the refrigerator for 3 or 4 days. While most commonly used in soup, *farro* makes a great salad—sort of a rustic tabbouleh.

To cook the *farro:* In a saucepan, combine the *farro*, water, and salt and bring to a boil over medium heat. Reduce the heat to low, cover, and simmer until the grains are soft but still have some firmness in the center, about 20 minutes. Start checking for doneness after 15 minutes. If not all the water has been absorbed, simply drain the cooked *farro* in a sieve. Place the *farro* in a bowl and let cool.

Season the cooked *farro* with the olive oil, vinegar, and salt and pepper to taste, tossing to coat, then fold in the onion, bell pepper, and celery. Just before eating, add the chopped parsley and basil and mix well.

Variation: Double the amount of oil and vinegar and add ½ cup cooked white beans or lentils.

FARRO

½ cup *farro*, rinsed or soaked in cold water for 1 hour

2 cups water

1 teaspoon salt

¼ cup extra-virgin olive oil, or as needed

2 tablespoons red wine vinegar, or as needed

Salt and freshly ground black pepper

¼ cup chopped red onion, or to taste

¼ cup chopped red bell pepper

¼ cup chopped celery, fennel, or diced cucumber

2 tablespoons chopped fresh flat-leaf parsley

2 tablespoons chopped fresh basil or mint

SPINACH SALAD with VARIATIONS

While a leafy salad is refreshing, it won't fill me up. But it can be a base for other ingredients that bring bulk and flavor to the mix. One of my favorite salad greens is baby spinach. Its mild flavor makes it hospitable to any number of embellishments and vinaigrettes, so I need never be bored. One day I might enjoy a Greek-inspired oregano-and-garlic vinaigrette and another time a refreshing mint vinaigrette.

Select a vinaigrette. To make the Oregano-Garlic Vinaigrette: In a bowl, whisk together all of the ingredients, including salt and pepper to taste. To make the Mint Vinaigrette: Begin with a flavor infusion, combining 2 tablespoons of the lemon juice and the 2 tablespoons chopped mint in a small saucepan or sauté pan. Bring to a boil and remove from the heat. Let steep for about 10 minutes, then strain through a fine-mesh sieve into a small bowl. There will be 2 tablespoons in all. Add the remaining ingredients, including the ¼ cup chopped mint and the 1 tablespoon lemon juice, and whisk together.

If using beans, toss them in 2 tablespoons of the vinai-grette and leave to marinate for about 30 minutes. In a small bowl, marinate the onion in 1 tablespoon of the vinaigrette for about 15 minutes to soften it and lessen its bite.

If the spinach leaves are large, remove the stems and tear the leaves into smaller pieces. If using a large beet, cut it in half and then into ¼-inch-slices. Cut small beets into quarters or eighths.

In a large salad bowl, combine the spinach, marinated onions, beets, and the beans and shrimp, if using, with the remaining vinaigrette. Toss well and sprinkle with the olives and feta.

OREGANO-GARLIC VINAIGRETTE

⅓ cup extra-virgin olive oil

3 tablespoons red wine vinegar

½ teaspoon minced garlic

1 teaspoon dried oregano

Salt and freshly ground black pepper

MINT VINAIGRETTE

3 tablespoons fresh lemon juice

2 tablespoons chopped fresh mint, plus ¼ cup tightly packed chopped mint

½ cup extra-virgin olive oil

2 tablespoons red wine vinegar

½ teaspoon honey

½ teaspoon salt

½ cup cooked white or black beans or chickpeas (optional)

½ small red onion, thinly sliced

2 large handfuls of baby spinach

1 large or 2 small beets, cooked and peeled

6 ounces cooked shrimp (optional)

¼ cup Kalamata olives

4 ounces feta cheese, coarsely crumbled

EVAN'S BIRTHDAY CHICKPEA SALAD with RED PEPPERS, GRILLED TUNA, and MOROCCAN VINAIGRETTE

When my son, Evan, turned forty, I decided to throw a party. A small guest list quickly grew, and I asked some former sous-chefs to cook with me. We had a long debate about the perfect vinaigrette for this salad. Should it be vinegar or lemon juice based? How hot could it be? We tasted and tasted. The salad was such a hit that I now make it for myself. I often cook double the amount of chickpeas, as the balance can be added to soups, stews, or side dishes. What made this salad so pretty was the combination of black and beige chickpeas. I ordered the black ones by mail from Indian Harvest (www.indianharvest.com or 800-346-7032), and they made for a dramatic presentation. A grilled chicken breast, boned and skinned, can be used in place of the tuna.

CHICKPEAS

½ cup dried chickpeas, preferably a mixture of black and beige

½ small yellow onion

1 clove garlic

1 bay leaf

1 teaspoon salt

MOROCCAN VINAIGRETTE

¼ cup red wine vinegar

1 teaspoon ground cumin, toasted in a dry pan

¼ teaspoon cayenne pepper

½ teaspoon freshly ground black pepper

1 clove garlic, finely minced

½ cup olive oil

¼ cup chopped fresh cilantro

Salt

½ small red onion, diced

1 red bell pepper, seeded and diced

Salt and freshly ground black pepper

8 ounces fresh tuna fillet, grilled or broiled and cut into ½-inch-wide strips, or canned tuna, drained and broken up into large pieces

1 hard-boiled egg, halved (optional)

¼ cup Moroccan black or green olives

To cook the chickpeas: Pick over them and remove any stones or debris. Rinse well, put in a saucepan, and cover with 2 cups water. Bring to a boil, reduce the heat to medium, and cook for 2 minutes. Remove from the heat and let stand for 1 hour. Drain the beans and return them to the saucepan with fresh water to cover by about 2 inches. Add the onion, garlic, and bay leaf and bring to a boil over medium-high heat. Reduce the heat to low, add the salt, cover, and simmer until the beans are tender but not falling apart, about 40 minutes. Remove and discard the onion, garlic, and bay, then drain the beans and set aside.

continued

To make the Moroccan Vinaigrette: In a small bowl, combine the vinegar, cumin, cayenne, and black pepper. Add the garlic and then whisk in the oil and cilantro. Season to taste with salt.

In a bowl, toss together the chickpeas, red onion, and bell pepper with the vinaigrette and let marinate for a few hours. Taste and adjust the seasoning with salt and pepper. Top with the tuna and with the egg, if using. Scatter the olives over the salad.

Variation: I often make a white bean salad with tuna. In the classic Italian version, the dressed white beans are topped with high-quality canned tuna and chopped red onion. For a more upscale salad, you can add cooked shellfish such as shrimp or lobster. I like to serve the salad surrounded with wedges of ripe tomato on a platter. Canned white beans are acceptable in a pinch, but they must be well rinsed before use. Prepare the white bean salad as for this chickpea and tuna salad, but dress it with extra-virgin olive oil and red wine vinegar, adding chopped fresh basil or mint. Or try the Moroccan Vinaigrette if you are in a North African mood.

BLACK BEAN SALAD, LATIN AMERICAN STYLE

Glistening black beans, the white and yellow of the chopped egg, and the surrounding red of the tomatoes and green of the avocado make for a particularly attractive plate. The Latin American accent comes in with the cilantro and chile in the vinaigrette and the addition of avocado. The choice of ham is up to you. An air-cured ham such as *serrano* or prosciutto is gamier; baked ham is sweeter; and smoked ham adds yet another nuance of flavor. In summer, I add corn for an extra Latino beat.

½ cup dried black beans

½ teaspoon salt, plus more to taste

4 tablespoons olive oil

3 tablespoons diced red onion

1 clove garlic, finely minced

1 jalapeño chile, finely minced

2 tablespoons red wine vinegar or sherry vinegar

2 tablespoons chopped fresh cilantro, plus more for garnish

½ cup corn kernels, cooked (optional)

Freshly ground black pepper

4 ounces prosciutto, serrano ham, or baked or smoked ham, cut ⅛ inch thick and then cut crosswise into 1-by-¼-inch strips

1 hard-boiled egg, coarsely chopped

Ripe tomato wedges for garnish

½ avocado, peeled and diced or sliced for garnish

Pick over the beans and remove any stones or debris. Rinse well, put in a saucepan, and cover with 2 cups water. Bring to a boil, reduce the heat to medium and cook for 2 minutes. Remove from the heat and let stand for 1 hour. Drain the beans and return them to the saucepan with fresh water to cover by 2 inches. Bring to a boil over medium-high heat. Reduce the heat to low, add the ½ teaspoon salt, cover, and simmer until tender but not falling apart, 45 to 60 minutes. Drain the beans and transfer to a large bowl. Toss with 2 tablespoons of the olive oil to coat and let cool.

When the beans have cooled, add the remaining 2 tablespoons oil, the onion, garlic, chile, vinegar, and 2 tablespoons cilantro and toss to coat and combine. Fold in the corn, if using. Season to taste with salt and pepper. I like these a bit peppery.

Transfer the beans to a deep platter or wide, shallow bowl. Sprinkle the ham and egg on top. Don't fold them in until you are ready to sit down and eat. Garnish with chopped cilantro and surround with the tomato and avocado.

LEBANESE FATTOUSH

When I had Square One Restaurant, *fattoush* was the most requested summer salad. The staff and customers would start asking for it in late June, and I would hold off until the tomatoes were perfect, ripe and perfumed. While this portion of *fattoush* can fill you up, you can extend the salad by adding cooked chicken or lamb or even a few shrimp.

1 large or 2 small pita breads

⅔ cup diced tomato (½-inch dice)

½ cup diced cucumber (½-inch dice), peeled and seeded if necessary

2 tablespoons very finely diced red onion

2 tablespoons finely chopped green onion, including tender green tops

2 tablespoons chopped fresh mint

¼ cup chopped fresh flat-leaf parsley

⅓ cup pure olive oil

¼ cup fresh lemon juice

½ teaspoon ground sumac (optional)

Salt and freshly ground black pepper

4 to 5 ounces sliced or diced cooked chicken or lamb or cooked shrimp (optional)

1 cup loosely packed romaine lettuce strips (1½ inches wide)

½ cup chopped purslane (optional)

Preheat the oven to 350°F. Place the pita breads on a baking sheet and bake until dry, about 15 minutes. Remove from the oven and, when cool enough to handle, break into bite-size pieces.

In a large salad bowl, combine the tomato, cucumber, red onion, green onion, mint, and parsley.

In a small bowl, whisk together the olive oil, lemon juice, the sumac, if using, and salt and pepper to taste.

If using chicken, add to the salad bowl and pour in half of the vinaigrette. Toss to mix. Then add the pita pieces, the romaine, the purslane, if using, and the remaining vinaigrette and toss to coat evenly.

DUCK and BELGIAN ENDIVE SALAD with PEAR

I think it's always best to let the salad components, except for the greens, macerate in some of the dressing so that they absorb the flavors and distribute them evenly throughout the mixture. It may mean washing a few extra small bowls, but the flavor impact is worth it.

BALSAMIC ORANGE VINAIGRETTE

2 tablespoons walnut oil

¼ cup pure olive oil

2 tablespoons balsamic vinegar or sherry vinegar

1 tablespoon minced shallot

Grated zest of 1 orange

2 tablespoons fresh orange juice (optional)

Salt and freshly ground black pepper

Slices of cooked roast duck (page 130) or duck breast (page 134)

1 small Anjou or Comice pear, halved, cored, and sliced

2 tablespoons walnuts, toasted

1 head Belgian endive, leaves separated

1 small head frisée, leaves separated

To make the vinaigrette: In a bowl whisk together the oils, vinegar, shallot, orange zest, and the orange juice, if using. Season to taste with salt and pepper.

Put the sliced duck in a small bowl and toss with a little of the vinaigrette. Place the pear slices in another small bowl or on a small plate and drizzle with some of the dressing. In yet another small bowl, toss the walnuts in a little of the vinaigrette. Let the duck, pear, and walnuts stand for 5 to 10 minutes.

Place the endive and frisée leaves in a salad bowl. Drizzle with the remaining vinaigrette and toss to coat. Add the duck, pear slices, and walnuts and toss again.

ASIAN-INSPIRED STEAK SALADS

MUSTARD-and-GINGER DRESSING

1 tablespoon Dijon mustard

1 1/2 tablespoons peeled and grated fresh ginger

1 1/2 tablespoons red wine vinegar

1 tablespoon soy sauce

1 teaspoon brown sugar

1/2 cup pure olive oil

KOREAN DRESSING

1 large clove garlic

1 1/2-inch piece fresh ginger, peeled and thinly sliced

1/2 teaspoon granulated sugar

2 tablespoons rice vinegar

1 tablespoon Dijon mustard or Russian Hot-and-Sweet Mustard (page 29)

1 tablespoon soy sauce

1/3 cup canola oil

1 tablespoon Asian sesame oil

6 to 8 ounces cooked steak, sliced 1/4 inch thick

2 or 3 small potatoes, boiled and sliced 1/4 inch thick

1/4 cup sliced cucumber, peeled and seeded if necessary, or cooked green beans

1/2 red bell pepper, seeded and cut into narrow strips

Generous handful of watercress, baby spinach, or mizuna

Toasted sesame seeds and chopped green onion, if using Korean Dressing

I love a good steak, but I find it so rich and filling that I rarely finish one. My favorite cuts are rib eye, hanger, and skirt. Rather than fire up the broiler or grill, I sear them in a heavy cast-iron pan or on my ridged stove-top griddle. I like steak cooked quite rare and often make enough for a salad for the next day. Here are two of my favorite salads. Select the dressing that you want, then use half of it to marinate the steak before cooking it, if you like. Otherwise, use half of the dressing on the salad and refrigerate the remainder for up to a week to use on another salad.

Select a dressing to make. To make the Mustard-and-Ginger Dressing: In a small bowl, whisk together all of the ingredients. Or put the ingredients in a covered jar and shake until the sugar dissolves. To make the Korean Dressing: Put the garlic and ginger in a mini-processor and process until you have a paste. (Or grind to a paste in a mortar with a pestle.) Add the sugar and vinegar and pulse to combine. Transfer to a small bowl and whisk in the mustard and soy sauce. Then whisk in the canola and sesame oils.

If you are using the dressing to marinate the steak, pour off half the dressing, then marinate the steak for up to 4 hours, cook as desired, and eat half of it hot. If not, reserve half of the dressing for another use.

To assemble the salad, in a large bowl, combine the sliced steak, potatoes, cucumber, bell pepper, greens, and salad dressing and toss together. Or arrange all of the components on a plate and drizzle the dressing on top. If you have used the Korean Dressing, sprinkle with sesame seeds and green onion.

RUSSIAN CHICKEN SALAD with SOUR CREAM DRESSING

This salad reflects my Russian heritage. Fortunately, its assertive ingredients—radishes, cucumbers, capers, cornichons—are tempered by the sour cream, chicken, potatoes, cooling romaine, and accompanying slices of dark rye.

To make the dressing: In a small bowl, whisk together the sugar, salt, pepper, lemon juice, and mustard. Whisk in the sour cream, then fold in the dill, capers, and cornichons. Adjust the seasoning with salt, pepper, and vinegar to taste. You should have 1 scant cup.

In a large salad bowl, combine the lettuce, cucumber, radish, green onion, potatoes, and chicken. Toss all with enough of the Sour Cream Dressing to coat the ingredients well. Garnish with the egg.

Note: See Pantry Sauces for other dressings for chicken salads such as Caesar Salad Dressing (page 35) and Chinese Chicken Salad Dressing (page 35).

SOUR CREAM DRESSING

1 teaspoon sugar

½ teaspoon salt, or to taste

½ teaspoon freshly ground black pepper, or to taste

2 tablespoons fresh lemon juice

2 tablespoons strong Dijon mustard

¾ cup sour cream

2 tablespoons chopped fresh dill

1 tablespoon chopped rinsed capers

1 tablespoon chopped cornichons

Distilled white vinegar

2 cups cut-up romaine leaves (2-inch pieces)

½ cup sliced or diced cucumber, peeled and seeded if necessary

¼ cup paper-thin radish slices

2 tablespoons finely chopped green onion, including tender green tops

2 or 3 small potatoes, boiled and sliced or diced

2 cups slivered or diced cooked chicken

1 hard-boiled egg, chopped

Pastas and **Grains**

Pastas and Grains

While I was assembling a list of recipes to include in this chapter, I realized that I could have devoted the entire book to pasta and grains for the solo diner. Pasta, rice, *farro,* or polenta can be the basis for a well-rounded meal. Each is inexpensive and easy to prepare, and single portions are always on hand in the basic pantry. Divide the pasta package in four and you have four solo suppers to be prepared whenever you have the urge. Cook up a half cup of rice, *farro,* or polenta and you have a satisfying dinner for one. Cook up a cup and you have great leftovers to play with for another meal.

Pastas and grains are the essence of what is known as comfort food. On their own, they are not sexy, but you can dress them up to make them irresistible. Although grains are neutral in taste, they are made lively with the addition of small amounts of meat, vegetables, or seafood—enhancements that can be frugal or deluxe. A few shrimp or some crabmeat can make a mundane meal a special-occasion dinner. On days when I am trying to cut back on animal protein, grains combined with vegetables provide immense culinary satisfaction.

POLENTA with SPINACH and PEAS

I usually eat this with a spoon directly from the pot. It is a quintessential comfort dish, and I make no apologies for my childish eating habits. This polenta and vegetable mixture could be served as a side dish with a simple piece of meat, fish, or poultry. But why bother when it is so satisfying on its own? By the way, I do not use instant polenta because I find the texture too smooth and uninteresting—like baby food. I prefer the crunchiness of a coarser-grain polenta, such as Golden Pheasant or Giusto's brand. But if you like a smoother polenta, use the instant. We all like to be babied from time to time.

1/3 cup coarse-grain polenta

1 1/2 cups water

1 teaspoon salt, plus more to taste

1/2 cup chopped cooked spinach, broccoli, or chard

1/4 cup cooked fresh or thawed frozen English peas

1/4 cup mascarpone cheese or 2 tablespoons unsalted butter

1 to 2 tablespoons grated Parmesan cheese

Combine the polenta and water in a small saucepan. Slowly bring to a boil over medium heat, whisking from time to time to break up any lumps that may form. Add the 1 tablespoon salt, reduce the heat to low, and simmer, stirring occasionally, until the polenta is thick, pulls away from the sides of the pan, and is no longer grainy on the tongue, 20 to 30 minutes.

Stir in the spinach, peas, mascarpone, and Parmesan. Taste and adjust with more salt. Eat with a spoon.

Note: If desired, double the polenta and pour the excess (with or without vegetables) into a lightly oiled baking dish. Refrigerate until ready to eat. Then, for a second meal, you can reheat it in the oven or microwave and top it with tomato sauce; or cut it into triangles or rectangles, sauté them in butter or oil, and top with tomato sauce; or dice it and add it to soup.

Variation: Instead of adding peas and spinach to the soft polenta, fold in 3/4 cup mashed cooked butternut squash or sweet potatoes and eat as is or serve as a side dish.

SPAGHETTI alla CARBONARA

4 ounces pancetta, cut into
¼-inch-thick slices

1 whole egg or 2 egg yolks

About 3 tablespoons grated
Parmesan cheese or part pecorino
and part Parmesan

About ½ teaspoon freshly ground
black pepper

1 tablespoon salt

4 ounces spaghetti

2 teaspoons unsalted butter

2 teaspoons olive oil

I ate *spaghetti alla carbonara* for the first time in Rome in the late 1950s, and my reaction to it was much like the reaction my granddaughter, Elena, had when she tasted her first lobster. I went crazy. I had to know how to make it. I ate it every week for months, sampling versions in any number of Roman trattorias to see which one made the best. I had lengthy discussions with Italians about the proper ratio of pancetta (actually Romans prefer *guanciale*, the pig's cheek, but that cut is not imported here), and if it should be allowed to crisp. How much black pepper? Should the cheese be Parmesan or part Parmesan and part pecorino? I tried three different brands of pancetta before settling on my favorite. Because our supermarket eggs do not have the flavor or the golden yolks of Roman eggs, I occasionally add an extra yolk to the mixture. Yes, I realize that this is a high-cholesterol special, but I don't care. I only eat this pasta once or twice a year. The rest of the time I am a model of Mediterranean dietary restraint.

Unroll the pancetta slices and cut them crosswise into ¼-inch-wide strips. In a large bowl, whisk together the egg, cheese, and pepper. If possible, keep the bowl near the stove or atop a warming shelf.

Bring a large pot of water to a boil. Drop in the salt and then the pasta. Stir well.

Spaghetti alla Carbonara

For the first time in eighteen years, I did not have to work on New Year's Eve. What a luxury to be able to stay home! I had been invited to two parties, but frankly I was not in the mood to make small talk. I wanted to unwind and relax in the comfort of my own nest. Having endured New Year's Eve in the restaurant business for so long, I now believe that New Year's Eve is an ideal night to stay home and perhaps, if feeling sociable, have a few friends over for dinner.

Now all I had to do was decide how to spend the evening and what I wanted to eat at my very private party. I began to think about the foods that make me feel festive. I developed a game plan for the evening based on a nostalgic scenario. Having spent some of the happiest times of my life in Rome, I decided to rent two of my favorite Italian movies (Mario Monicelli's *I soliti ignoti*, known in the United States as *Big Deal on Madonna Street*, and Federico Fellini's *8 ½*), open a bottle of Brunello from my cellar, and make *spaghetti alla carbonara*. I do not agree with Calvin Trillin when he says this famed pasta should replace turkey as the official Thanksgiving entrée, only because I love cooking the Thanksgiving meal. I do agree, however, that it is a most celebratory dish. Why, you might ask, since the ingredients are rather mundane? It's almost breakfast: pancetta, eggs, cheese, and black pepper tossed with pasta. But executed with finesse and perfect timing, it is sublime.

Spaghetti alla carbonara also falls into the category of comfort food. I was feeling festive, but also in need of comfort and familiarity. So *carbonara* it was, along with a lovely endive and watercress salad to offer some relief from the pasta's richness.

While the pasta is cooking, in a sauté pan, melt the butter with the olive oil over medium heat. Add the pancetta and cook, stirring occasionally, until bubbles appear in the pan, 5 to 7 minutes. The pancetta will be cooked but not crisp.

When the pasta is al dente, drain and add to the bowl with the egg mixture. Immediately add the pancetta and most of the drippings, and toss very quickly to combine. The sauce should be a thick, creamy liquid. Add additional cheese and pepper, if desired. Eat while hot. This pasta does not reheat, so make just enough.

Variation with Peas, Broccoli, or Asparagus: To feel less guilty about the cholesterol intake, you can add something green to this pasta. Even though it is not authentic, it looks pretty, tastes good, and makes you feel as if you are eating a more healthful pasta. Peas, broccoli, or asparagus are a good addition. Parboil ½ cup English peas, a small handful of broccoli florets, or ½ cup cut-up asparagus (1-inch pieces) in boiling salted water until sweet and tender-firm, a minute or so. Drain and refresh in cold water, then drain again and pat dry. When the pasta is a minute or two away from being al dente, drop the vegetables into the pasta pot to warm through quickly. Drain the pasta and vegetables and add to the egg mixture along with the pancetta and toss well.

RIGATONI with EGGPLANT, MEATBALLS, and TOMATO SAUCE

Generations of Italian-Americans have been embarrassed by the clichéd image of a bowl of spaghetti and one or two giant meatballs. They've been told it's not really Italian. I say there is no reason to be ashamed of meatballs. In fact, a meatball tradition exists in the Abruzzo, Apulia, and Calabria. They are not those leaden giants, however, but rather small, delicate *polpette* that appear in broth, layered in lasagna, or tossed with pasta. Here they are combined with sautéed cubes of eggplant, tomato sauce, and a few dollops of fresh ricotta. And if I am cutting back on meat, I make this pasta with just eggplant and tomatoes, adding bits of fresh ricotta or diced fresh mozzarella for texture. This recipe yields two portions, one to serve for supper and one to reheat as a gratin for another meal.

MEATBALLS

8 ounces ground beef or part beef and part pork

¼ cup grated onion

1 clove garlic, very finely minced

1 tablespoon mixed herbs, including chopped fresh thyme, sage, and flat-leaf parsley and dried oregano

Salt and freshly ground black pepper

1 medium eggplant, peeled and cut into 1-inch cubes

1 tablespoon salt, plus more for the eggplant

¼ cup pure olive oil, or as needed

1½ cups tomato sauce

8 ounces rigatoni, preferably De Cecco brand

½ cup ricotta cheese

Chopped fresh flat-leaf parsley for garnish

Grated Parmesan cheese for serving

To make the meatballs: In a bowl, combine the ground meat, onion, garlic, herbs, and a little salt and pepper. Fry a tiny patty of the mixture to see if it is seasoned to your taste. Adjust the seasoning, if necessary, then form the mixture into meatballs about 1 inch in diameter. You want about 2 dozen. Refrigerate the meatballs until ready to fry.

Sprinkle the eggplant with salt and let it sit in a colander for 30 minutes. Wipe dry with a dish towel or paper towels. In a large sauté pan, heat the ¼ cup olive oil over medium-high heat. Quickly cook the eggplant cubes, stirring often until they are golden on all sides, about 5 minutes. With a slotted spoon, transfer to a plate.

Add more olive oil to the pan as needed to form a film, and fry the meatballs, in batches, over medium-high heat until they are brown on the outside but still a bit rare in the center, about 8 minutes. Drain them on paper towels.

In a wide sauté pan, heat the tomato sauce over medium heat. Add the meatballs and eggplant and reduce the heat to very low to keep them hot. Bring a large pot of water to a boil. Add the 1 tablespoon salt and then the pasta. Stir well and cook until al dente. Drain well and mix with the sauce and meatballs, tossing in dollops of the ricotta at the same time. Combine swiftly.

Spoon half of this dish into a warmed bowl. Garnish it with parsley and a little Parmesan cheese and eat immediately. Spoon the remaining half into an oiled individual gratin dish. Cover and refrigerate for a few days or freeze for up to 2 months. To reheat, preheat the oven to 350°F. Top with Parmesan and bake until heated through, about 15 minutes. Alternatively, place in the microwave until heated.

FARRO with BUTTERNUT SQUASH and CHESTNUTS

Cultivated in western Tuscany, in the area known as the Garfagnana, and in the Abruzzo to the east, *farro* is an early variety of wheat. The grain is semipearled, which means that some of the outer coating still remains after a few abrasions. Lighter in mouth-feel than wheat berries, *farro* has a taste and texture that resembles barley more than wheat. The kernels from the Garfagnana cook a bit more quickly than those from the Abruzzo because they are more pearled, so that less of the outer hull remains. Although many *farro* recipes tell you to soak the grain, I find this unnecessary. The pearled *farro* from the Garfagnana cooks in about 20 minutes. The sturdier, browner *farro* from the Abruzzo takes about 30 minutes and may be soaked for 30 minutes if you want it to cook a bit more quickly.

Cooked *farro* reheats like a dream in a little broth or water and holds well in the refrigerator for up to 5 days. I must confess that I am addicted to it and could eat it every day for a week. I usually make enough *farro* for a few days as it keeps well. The following recipe for basic *farro* will yield enough for two meals. For an easy second meal, add the kernels from an ear of corn, a little broth, a pat of butter, and salt and pepper. Like risotto, *farro* can be enhanced with leftover cooked chicken and sautéed mushrooms, or sautéed mushrooms and toasted hazelnuts.

BASIC FARRO

4 cups water

2 teaspoons salt

1 cup *farro*

½ cup vegetable or chicken stock, or a bit more for a soupier dish

2 tablespoons olive oil or 1 tablespoon each olive oil and unsalted butter

½ small onion, chopped

1 teaspoon chopped fresh sage

½ cup cubed, peeled butternut squash (½-inch cubes), boiled until al dente

4 or 5 cooked chestnuts, cut into bite-size pieces

2 tablespoons unsalted butter

Salt and freshly ground black pepper

continued

In a saucepan, bring the water to a boil. Add the salt and then the *farro*, stir, reduce the heat, cover, and simmer until the grains are soft but still have some firmness at the center. Start checking for doneness after 20 minutes. If not all of the water has been absorbed, simply drain the cooked *farro* in a sieve. Set aside 1 cup cooked *farro*, or a bit more for a heartier dish, and then cover and refrigerate the remainder for another dish such as soup or salad.

Pour the stock into a saucepan and bring to a simmer. Meanwhile, in a deep sauté pan, heat the olive oil over medium heat. Add the onion and sage and sauté until tender, 8 to 10 minutes. Add the *farro*, squash, chestnuts, and the hot stock. Stir gently and simmer over low heat until the *farro*, squash, and chestnuts are heated through and some of the stock has been absorbed, just a few minutes. Stir in the 2 tablespoons butter, season to taste with salt and pepper, and spoon into a warmed bowl.

RISOTTO with MUSHROOMS, PEAS, and GREMOLATA

2 cups chicken or vegetable stock

3 tablespoons unsalted butter or olive oil

¼ cup chopped onion

½ cup Italian short-grain rice

6 ounces assorted fresh mushrooms, wiped clean and sliced ¼ inch thick

¼ cup cooked fresh or thawed frozen English peas (see introduction)

2 tablespoons chopped fresh flat-leaf parsley

2 teaspoons minced garlic

2 teaspoons grated fresh lemon zest

Salt and freshly ground black pepper

Grated Parmesan cheese for serving (optional)

Risotto is comfort food. Warm and slightly soupy, it can be eaten with a spoon if you are feeling too lazy to eat it with a fork. It is a great vehicle for using up leftovers (being thrifty is a comfort in itself). Bits of cooked chicken or turkey or some chopped prosciutto would make a nice addition. If you can find flavorful, nonstarchy fresh English peas, by all means use them. About 4 ounces unshelled will give you ¼ cup shelled peas. Cook them in boiling salted water until tender, drain, and refresh in cold water. If they are unavailable, use thawed frozen peas. If you can find wild mushrooms and are feeling financially flush, buy a few to add to the more mundane whites or browns. *Gremolata* is a traditional garnish added to ossobuco but it also is a great addition to risotto. It is a mixture of parsley, garlic, and grated lemon zest.

When making risotto, remember to keep the stock at a constant simmer and add it in small amounts only after the previous additions have been absorbed by the rice. You will need Italian short-grain rice such as arborio or carnaroli, as it will absorb liquid gradually yet remain al dente in the center. Risotto cannot be rushed and needs to be stirred from time to time. I find that the ritual of making it is just as comforting as eating it. Any leftover risotto can be reheated in the microwave or thinned with stock and served as a soup.

Pour the stock into a saucepan and bring to a boil over high heat. Adjust the heat to maintain a very low simmer. Heat 1 tablespoon of the butter in a large sauté pan with high sides or a shallow saucepan over medium heat. Add the onion and cook until translucent and soft, about 8 minutes. Add the rice and cook, stirring often, until the rice is opaque, about 3 minutes. Ladle in ½ cup of the hot stock and simmer over low heat, stirring occasionally, until the stock is absorbed. Add about ½ cup more stock and continue to cook and stir over low heat until the stock is absorbed. Continue to add stock in the same manner until the rice is almost al dente.

While the rice is cooking, heat the remaining 2 tablespoons butter in a large sauté pan and quickly cook the mushrooms over high heat, stirring often, until tender. This will take about 4 minutes.

When the rice is almost done, add the mushrooms and peas and continue to cook until most of the liquid has been absorbed and the rice is al dente but still firm in the center and the mixture is creamy. Stir together the parsley, garlic, and lemon zest to make the *gremolata* and then stir it into the risotto. Season to taste with salt and pepper. Transfer to a warmed bowl and sprinkle with Parmesan, if desired.

ORECCHIETTE with BROCCOLI and CHICKPEAS

1/2 cup dried chickpeas or white beans

4 teaspoons salt, plus more to taste

2 tablespoons extra-virgin olive oil, plus more for drizzling

1 generous cup broccoli florets or broccoli rabe

3 to 4 ounces orecchiette

4 tablespoons minced red onion (optional)

1 tablespoon minced garlic

1/2 teaspoon red pepper flakes (optional)

1 cup diced canned plum tomatoes (optional)

Freshly ground black pepper

2 tablespoons Toasted Bread Crumbs (optional)

Grated pecorino cheese for serving (optional)

Orecchiette with beans, greens, garlic, and chile is one of my standby suppers. The pasta itself is fun to eat. The name translates as "little ears," but to me the pasta shells resemble little belly buttons, the central dimple of which is ideal for trapping the beans. Sometimes I use bitter broccoli rabe, blanched and coarsely chopped. Sometimes I use broccoli or romanesco broccoli florets. Toasted Bread Crumbs (page 82) may or may not go into the mix. Grated pecorino may garnish the dish. I've even been known to add crabmeat, steamed clams, shrimp, meatballs, or sausage to the basic mixture of beans, greens, and pasta. Simply put, this dish offers versatility in a bowl, satisfying in its simplest form, and hospitable to other flavors.

Pick over the chickpeas and remove any stones or debris. Rinse well, put in a saucepan and cover with 2 cups water. Bring to a boil, reduce the heat to medium and cook for 2 minutes. Remove from the heat and let stand for 1 hour. Drain the chickpeas and return them to the saucepan with fresh water to cover by 2 inches. Bring to a boil over medium-high heat. Reduce the heat to low, add 2 teaspoons of the salt, cover, and cook until tender but not falling apart, about 40 minutes. Drain and transfer to a bowl. Drizzle with a bit of olive oil. (You may also use canned chickpeas or white beans, drained and rinsed, but their texture is softer than those you cook yourself.)

continued

Bring a large pot of water to a boil. Add the remaining 2 teaspoons salt and then drop in the broccoli and cook until tender but not too soft, 4 to 5 minutes. Remove with a slotted spoon and refresh in cold water to set the color. Drain and set aside. If using broccoli rabe, chop coarsely. Then drop the orecchiette into the same boiling salted water.

While the pasta cooks, in a sauté pan, heat the 2 tablespoons olive oil over medium heat. Add the onion, if using, and cook until tender, about 8 minutes. Add the garlic, red pepper flakes (if using), and chickpeas and cook for 2 minutes. Add the tomatoes (if using) and broccoli and cook until hot. Season to taste with salt and pepper.

Drain the pasta when it is al dente and add it to the broccoli sauce, along with the toasted bread crumbs, if using. Warm through. Transfer to a warmed bowl and sprinkle with pecorino, if desired.

Toasted Bread Crumbs: Heat the oven to 350°F. In a food processor, pulse 2 cups diced country-style bread, crusts removed, until you have coarse crumbs. Toss the crumbs in a bowl with 4 tablespoons (1/2 stick) unsalted butter, melted, or olive oil; 1 teaspoon salt; and 1/2 teaspoon freshly ground black pepper. Spread the crumbs on a baking sheet. Bake, stirring occasionally, until golden, about 20 minutes. The crumbs can be stored in the pantry in a covered container for up to a month.

PAPPARDELLE with CHICKEN LIVERS

When I lived in Rome, every week I patronized a wonderful small restaurant called Alfredo alla Chiesa Nuova. On the piazza in front of the restaurant was this hilarious fountain that looked like a giant soup tureen with two small spouts at either end, each giving off a tiny trickle of water. Sadly, I have gone back only to find that while the fountain remains, the restaurant is no longer in existence.

This chicken liver pasta was one of my Chiesa Nuova favorites. Sometimes the cooks added pancetta or prosciutto, sautéed mushrooms, or tomato purée.

If you are using dried pasta, you can drop it in the water about 12 minutes before you are ready to eat. Fresh pasta takes only a few minutes to cook, so you will probably want to make the sauce, then drop in the noodles.

6 ounces chicken livers

4 or 5 ounces fresh or dried *pappardelle* or dried rigatoni

1 tablespoon salt, plus more to taste

2 tablespoons pure olive oil

½ small red onion, sliced ¼ inch thick

2 fresh sage leaves

1 tablespoon unsalted butter

Freshly ground black pepper

⅓ cup chicken stock

2 tablespoons dry Marsala or dry white wine

1 or 2 tablespoons tomato paste (optional)

¼ cup sautéed mushrooms (about 3 large; optional)

2 tablespoons diced prosciutto (optional)

Trim the livers of all fat and connective tissue. Cut away any greenish spots.

Bring a large pot of water to a boil. If you are using dried pasta, add the tablespoon of salt and then the pasta now. Stir well and cook until al dente. If you are using fresh pasta, add the salt and pasta when the sauce is almost done and cook until tender.

In a sauté pan, heat 1 tablespoon of the olive oil over high heat. Cook the onion and sage leaves until the onion is softened and golden, about 10 minutes. Transfer to a plate.

Heat the remaining 1 tablespoon oil and the butter in the same pan over high heat. Add the livers and quickly sear on all sides. Sprinkle with salt and pepper. Return the onion and sage to the pan and add the chicken stock, wine, and the tomato paste to taste, if using, and bring to a boil. Add the mushrooms and prosciutto, if using, and heat through.

Drain the pasta, add to the sauté pan, and toss well. Heat for 1 minute and turn out into a warmed bowl.

LINGUINE alle VONGOLE

18 to 20 small manila or other small clams or about 12 larger clams, well scrubbed

⅓ cup dry white wine

1 tablespoon salt, plus more to taste

4 or 5 ounces dried linguine

2 tablespoons extra-virgin olive oil

1 to 2 teaspoons finely minced garlic

Pinch of dried oregano (optional)

Pinch of red pepper flakes (optional)

1 to 2 tablespoons chopped fresh flat-leaf parsley

Freshly ground black pepper

1 to 2 tablespoons extra-virgin olive oil or unsalted butter

While I do enjoy digging into a bowl of steamed clams, they do not fill me up for supper unless I eat lots of bread. I guess that is why they are offered as a first course in most restaurants. For my solo suppers I don't usually prepare multiple courses. The perfect solution to a clam (or mussel) craving is pasta. Linguine with clams and lots of garlic is one of my favorites.

When you order pasta with clams in Italy, the clams are usually served in the shell. They are tiny—the size of a quarter—and part of the pleasure of eating them is to remove each clam with a small fork and then twirl it in the pasta. Some people find this messy and would rather not deal with the shells, and it may be difficult to find tiny clams at the market. If all you can find are the large ones, you will still have a delicious dish. Steam the clams, chop them, cover them with the strained clam juices, and add them to the pasta sauce. If you can find small ones, leave them in the shell for an authentic touch. Mussels can be substituted; steam and shell them but leave them whole.

In a large sauté pan, combine the clams and white wine. Bring to a boil, cover, and steam until the clams open. This can happen quickly, 3 to 4 minutes for small clams, or 5 to 7 minutes if the clams are large and stubborn. As soon as they have opened, remove them from the pan, discarding any that have failed to open. Strain the pan juices through a cheesecloth-lined sieve placed over a bowl. If the clams are large, when they are cool enough to handle, remove them from their shells and chop into bite-size pieces. If they are small, you may prefer to keep them in the shells. Put the the clams in the bowl with the strained broth.

Bring a large pot of water to a boil. Drop in the 1 tablespoon salt and then the pasta. Stir well and cook until al dente.

While the pasta cooks, in a medium sauté pan, heat the olive oil over medium heat. Add the garlic to taste and the oregano and red pepper flakes, if using, and cook for a minute or two. Add the clams and their juices and heat through gently. Do not overcook or the clams will toughen. Add the parsley to taste and lots of black pepper. Season with salt if the clams are not salty enough. Swirl in the olive oil to enrich the pan juices.

Drain the linguine, add to the sauce, and toss well. Transfer to a warmed bowl.

Variation: You may add ½ cup diced, peeled, and seeded tomatoes or a spoonful of tomato sauce just before you add the clams. And/or you may add ½ cup chopped cooked broccoli or romanesco broccoli with the clams.

MACARONI and CHEESE, CLASSIC and BAROQUE

Macaroni and cheese is really a baked version of the Italian classic pasta *ai tre formaggi* (with three cheeses). Comfort food at it best, this familiar dish may be reheated or frozen and reheated, so why not make a double batch? To make the dish more festive, add crabmeat, lobster, diced cooked ham, or leftover meatballs (page 50). Cooked vegetables such as broccoli may also be added.

1 tablespoon salt, plus more to taste

6 ounces macaroni

1 tablespoon olive oil

3 or 4 tablespoons unsalted butter

2 tablespoons all-purpose flour

1 cup milk

¼ cup heavy cream

Freshly ground black pepper

Freshly grated nutmeg

¼ cup shredded Fontina or Emmentaler cheese

6 tablespoons grated Parmesan cheese

6 tablespoons grated white Cheddar cheese

¼ cup Toasted Bread Crumbs (page 82)

OPTIONAL ADDITIONS for EACH HALF PORTION

6 ounces lump crabmeat, picked over for shell fragments, or meat from 1 lobster (page 107) mixed with ½ cup cooked English peas and 1 tablespoon minced fresh chives

1 cup diced cooked ham, ½ cup cooked English peas, and 1 tablespoon minced fresh chives

1 cup cooked broccoli, sautéed mushrooms, or diced uncooked tomatoes

Butter 2 large ramekins or individual gratin dishes. Bring a large pot of water to a boil. Drop in the 1 tablespoon of salt and the pasta and cook until al dente. Drain, then rinse to stop the cooking. Transfer to a bowl, toss with the tablespoon of olive oil, and set aside.

In a saucepan, melt 2 tablespoons of the butter over medium heat. Stir in the flour and cook, stirring often, for 3 minutes. Add the milk and cream and bring to a boil. Reduce the heat to low and simmer, stirring occasionally, until thickened, about 5 minutes. Season to taste with salt, pepper, and nutmeg.

Add the sauce to the drained macaroni and fold in the Fontina and 4 tablespoons each of the Parmesan and Cheddar cheeses. Divide the mixture into 2 equal portions. If desired, select 1 of the optional additions (seafood, ham, or vegetable) to add to 1 portion, and leave the other plain, or flavor both portions, or leave both plain. Spoon a macaroni portion into each of the prepared dishes.

Divide the remaining 2 tablespoons of the Parmesan and Cheddar cheeses evenly between the dishes, sprinkling them over the surface. Then sprinkle on the bread crumbs, again dividing evenly. Cut the remaining 1 or 2 tablespoons of butter into small pieces and dot the top of each dish. Cover and refrigerate until ready to bake. The second portion may be refrigerated for up to 2 days or frozen for up to 1 month.

Bake in a preheated 400°F oven until bubbly and golden brown, 25 to 30 minutes. Eat piping hot.

Falling in Love with a New Food and Making It Your Own

Like most chefs, when I taste a new food, I hope it will be the beginning of a long love affair rather than a one-night stand. That's how it was for me and *farro*. This ancient wheat first caught my culinary attention at a conference in Turin sponsored by Slow Food, an international organization dedicated to maintaining traditional foods and sustainable agriculture. A trattoria from Lucca served a tasting dinner promoting regional specialties, among them *farro (Triticum dicoccum),* which is grown in the hills surrounding Lucca, an area known as the Garfagnana. Also erroneously known as emmer wheat or spelt, it had become an endangered crop, threatened with extinction, and local farmers were trying to bring it back to the table. At the dinner, the *farro* was a component in a hearty soup and in a filling for a rich tart. I liked it, but was not blown away. When I next encountered *farro,* it was served as a grain salad, dressed with extra-virgin olive oil. Finally I tasted it as a warm side dish, simple and elegant. I was captivated. I loved the chewy texture and nutty scent—reminiscent of barley but with more flavor. I was a woman on a mission. I needed to cook it often until I understood its properties so it could find a permanent home in my cooking repertoire. But few people were importing it and it was hard to find.

Some years later, when I was traveling in the Abruzzo, I visited a mill that grew and processed *farro.* I bought many bags to bring home. I cooked it and compared it to the Lucca version. It was a bit firmer but just as tasty. I cooked it as a pilaf, then as a risotto. I steamed it, reheated it, and added wild mushrooms. Then I tried adding chestnuts, then butternut squash, and even corn. Everything was good. I discovered that I liked it best with a knob of butter stirred in at the end. I was hooked. *Farro* has become a major comfort food for me, and I can blissfully eat it by the bowlful. Fortunately, *farro,* both from Tuscany and the Abruzzo, is now at a few Italian markets and even at my local supermarket in the Italian import section. Farro is available online at agferrari.com

A similar love affair occurred with romanesco broccoli, an early variety of broccoli, light green in color, with florets shaped in pointy whorls. I cooked the broccoli straight, then used it in pasta and soup, as a side dish, and in a gratin. Again I was hooked.

Then there was my fling with *pimentón,* Spanish paprika. I first tasted it in Barcelona. I tried to figure out why the paella tasted so deep and smoky. Then I thought I detected this smokiness in a *romesco* sauce. Again, a new flavor layer was revealed. Finally, I found the secret ingredient, a Spanish paprika called *pimentón de la Vera.* Like the Hungarian, it came sweet, semi-hot, or hot. But the Spanish peppers were dried over a smoldering wood fire, imparting a subtle smoky quality to the spice. I bought some and have been cooking with it ever since. My paella base has a deeper taste and my *romesco* sauce (page 22) has been transformed. Since Spain and Morocco are neighbors, I have added it to Moroccan *charmoula* marinade (page 111). I have also rubbed it on fish and lamb chops, and I am not done exploring all the options.

When you meet a new food, find a new taste that intrigues and pleases you, explore it, pursuing all the possibilities.

Eggs and **Cheese**

Eggs and Cheese

Like many well-prepared cooks, I always have eggs and cheese in the refrigerator. While they are most often used to enhance other recipes, they can also be instantly transformed into a quick solo supper. A cheese omelet is always an easy last-minute meal, while a frittata is an ideal way to use up leftover vegetables. So, too, is a savory bread pudding made with eggs, cheese, crumbled bread, and flavorful cooked vegetables such as broccoli, tomatoes, or asparagus. A grilled cheese sandwich or quesadilla can be a low-effort, high-comfort supper. If I am feeling more ambitious, I might sit down to a cheese soufflé or cheese pudding, sip a glass of fine wine, and celebrate my good fortune to be eating such an elegant dinner.

CHEESE SOUFFLÉ

When I was growing up and just becoming interested in fine cooking, I thought that soufflés were the essence of sophistication. Word was that they were difficult to prepare and were so fragile that they could collapse if someone coughed at the dining table. Now I know that they are simply a puffed omelet fortified with béchamel and not that tricky, although still elegant and delicious. I like the idea of bacon and chives with Gruyère, but prefer just chives with the goat cheese version. This is a sensual supper for one. Serve along with a salad of bitter greens such as endive or watercress, toasted walnuts, and apple slivers, dressed with walnut vinaigrette. And maybe a warm baguette.

1½ tablespoons unsalted butter

1½ tablespoons all-purpose flour

⅔ cup milk, warmed

Salt and freshly ground black pepper

2 eggs, separated, plus 1 egg white

2 ounces Gruyère cheese, shredded, or fresh goat cheese, crumbled

1 tablespoon minced fresh chives or green onion tops

1 slice bacon, cooked until crisp and crumbled, or 1 slice Canadian bacon or ham, diced (optional)

Preheat the oven to 425 degrees°F. Butter an oval 2-cup gratin dish or a small round soufflé dish.

In a saucepan, melt the butter over medium heat. Add the flour and stir well, reduce the heat to low, and cook, whisking, for about 3 minutes. Whisk in the milk, bring to a boil over medium heat, reduce the heat to low, and simmer, stirring, until thickened, about 6 minutes. Season to taste with salt and pepper. Lightly beat the yolks until blended, then slowly add to the milk mixture, stirring constantly. Transfer to a large bowl.

In another bowl, beat the egg whites until stiff peaks form. To the yolk mixture, add half of the cheese, the chives, the bacon, if using, and one-third of the egg whites and stir to combine. Then gently fold in the remaining whites, being careful not to deflate them. Spoon the mixture into the prepared dish and top with the remaining cheese.

Bake until the top is golden, about 15 minutes. It's all right if the center is a bit creamy and soft, rather than dry throughout. Eat at once.

ASPARAGUS with EGGS and PARMESAN CHEESE

8 ounces asparagus

1 tablespoon unsalted butter

1 or 2 thin slices prosciutto, preferably Parma or San Daniele (optional)

2 eggs

Freshly ground black pepper

2 tablespoons grated Parmesan cheese

I always look forward to the local asparagus season, which lasts from March until May. I eat the tender spears almost every day during this time, making too much (on purpose) so that I am left with asparagus to serve as a salad with a citrus or balsamic vinaigrette. Or I may incorporate the leftover spears in an omelet or frittata, pasta or risotto.

This dish is one of my favorite ways to prepare asparagus for a light supper (and it could be a great brunch, too). I have an asparagus steamer with a basket insert that allows the asparagus to cook standing up, thicker stems immersed in boiling water while the more delicate tops steam. But you can cook them in a deep saucepan and remove them carefully with tongs or a large wire skimmer.

Snap off the tough ends from the asparagus and peel the lower half of each stalk if they are thick. Bring a large saucepan of salted water to a boil. Add the asparagus and cook until just tender, 5 to 8 minutes, depending on thickness. Drain, refresh in cold water to set the color, and drain again. Pat dry with paper towels or a kitchen towel.

Preheat the oven to 450°F. Grease a small gratin dish with about 1 teaspoon of the butter. Arrange the asparagus spears, tips facing in the same direction, in the prepared dish. If using the prosciutto, you may divide the spears into 2 bundles, or leave them in a single one, and wrap in a thin slice of prosciutto. Or you can dice the prosciutto and sprinkle it over the asparagus. Break the eggs over the asparagus and then sprinkle with some pepper and the Parmesan cheese. (You won't need salt, as the cheese and prosciutto are rather salty.) Cut the remaining butter into bits and use it to dot the eggs and asparagus evenly.

Place in the oven and bake until the whites are set and yolks are still runny, 8 to 10 minutes. Eat piping hot.

BLINTZES

Who knew they were crepes? When I was growing up in New York, these were called blintzes. I still love them and have come to appreciate the versatility of the basic vehicle, the crepe. Over the years I have stuffed crepes with a variety of fillings—curried seafood, sautéed mushrooms, warm apple slices—and have even made the famed crêpes suzette. But none satisfies me more than a blintze. The classic is filled with farmer or cottage cheese, perfumed with cinnamon and raisins. Warm, crusty, served with a dollop of good sour cream or crème fraîche, one bite and I am transported back to my childhood. Blintzes freeze beautifully, so I usually double the recipe and then thaw them before sautéing. For variety, you can fill blintzes with seasoned mashed potatoes or meat. If you use an 8-inch sauté pan, and every crepe comes out well, you will have 4 or 5 crepes.

CREPE BATTER

1 egg

⅓ cup milk

¼ cup water

½ cup all-purpose flour

Pinch of salt

1 tablespoon unsalted butter, melted

Unsalted butter for cooking crepes and frying blintzes

Filling of choice (pages 95–96)

To make the crepe batter: In a bowl, whisk together the egg, milk, water, flour, salt, and melted butter. Alternatively, combine the ingredients in a blender and process until smooth. Let the batter rest for at least 30 minutes or for up to 4 hours in the refrigerator before using.

Melt 2 tablespoons or so of butter for cooking the crepes. Place a crepe pan over medium heat and lightly brush with melted butter. Ladle in 2 or 3 tablespoons of batter and swirl the pan to coat with a thin film of batter. Cook until the crepe is set on the first side, about 1 minute, then turn it with your fingers. Cook until barely set on the second side, less than a minute. Do not let the crepe color, although the edges may brown a bit. Slide it onto a clean towel, then butter the pan again and repeat until all of the batter is used.

Select a filling to make. Place a generous ¼ cup of the filling in the center of each crepe. Fold up the sides, then fold the top over the bottom. Arrange 2 blintzes, seam-side down, on a dish, cover well and place in the refrigerator until you are ready to fry them. They will keep for up to 2 days. Wrap the remaining 2 blintzes and place in the freezer for up to 1 month. Thaw the blintzes fully before sautéing.

To cook the blintzes, in a sauté pan, melt 2 tablespoons butter over medium heat. When it is bubbling, add the 2 blintzes and sauté, turning once, until golden on both sides, about 5 minutes total. Serve the blintzes warm, topping as suggested.

To make the potato filling: Preheat the oven to 450°F. Pierce the potatoes with the tines of a fork, place in the oven, and bake until tender when squeezed with a pot holder–covered hand or tested with a knife, about 1 hour. When cool enough to handle, cut in half, scoop out the flesh from the skins and, while still warm, pass through a ricer or mash with a fork. You should have about 1¼ cups of potato. The texture should be somewhat rough.

In a sauté pan, melt the chicken fat over medium heat. Add the onion and cook until tender and pale gold, about 10 minutes. Fold the onion into the potatoes, add the egg yolk and the smoked salmon, if using, and season with salt, pepper, and parsley. (The filling may be made a day ahead.) Serve the blintzes hot or warm, topping them with sour cream.

POTATO FILLING

2 large russet potatoes

2 tablespoons rendered chicken fat or unsalted butter

1 small onion, finely chopped

1 egg yolk

¼ cup diced smoked salmon (optional)

1 teaspoon salt

1 teaspoon freshly ground black pepper

2 tablespoons chopped fresh flat-leaf parsley

Sour cream for serving

continued

MEAT FILLING

1 tablespoon olive oil

¼ cup chopped onion

1 clove garlic, minced

⅛ teaspoon freshly grated nutmeg

½ teaspoon chopped fresh thyme

8 ounces ground beef

2 tablespoons chopped fresh flat-leaf parsley

1 egg

3 tablespoons dried bread crumbs

Salt and freshly ground black pepper

Sour cream and chopped fresh chives for serving

To make the meat filling: In a large sauté pan, heat the olive oil over medium heat. Add the onion and sauté until tender, 8 to 10 minutes. Add the garlic, nutmeg, and thyme and sauté for 1 minute. Add the beef and cook over medium-high heat, stirring often, until the meat is lightly browned, about 5 minutes.

Remove from the heat and stir in the parsley, egg, and bread crumbs. Season with salt and lots of pepper and let the mixture cool before filling the crepes. Although it doesn't pass the kosher test, I like to serve these with a dollop of sour cream and a sprinkling of chives.

CHEESE FILLING

1 cup creamed small-curd cottage cheese or fromage blanc

¼ cup golden raisins, plumped in hot water

1 ½ tablespoons sugar

1 teaspoon grated lemon zest

¼ teaspoon ground cinnamon

1 egg yolk (optional)

Sour cream, berries, or confectioners' or granulated sugar for serving

To make the cheese filling: In a bowl, combine the cheese, raisins, sugar, lemon zest, cinnamon, and the egg yolk, if using. Mix well. Serve the blintzes with a dollop of sour cream, a sprinkling of berries, or a dusting of sugar.

VEGETABLE BREAD PUDDING

This is a delectable cross between a frittata, a gratin, and a bread pudding. During the summer and early fall, I like to use fresh tomatoes and zucchini. When tomatoes are out of season, I might use canned tomatoes or substitute mashed roasted eggplant. I select herbs for taste harmony. Tomatoes and zucchini are enhanced by fresh basil. Zucchini and eggplant do well with dill or mint.

12 ounces ripe tomatoes, peeled, seeded, and chopped

Salt

Sugar

8 ounces zucchini, grated

1 slice rustic bread, crust removed, soaked in water, then squeezed dry

2 eggs

2 tablespoons chopped fresh basil or flat-leaf parsley

¼ cup ricotta cheese

½ cup shredded Gruyère or Swiss cheese

2 tablespoons grated Parmesan cheese

Freshly ground black pepper

Place the tomatoes in a colander and sprinkle with salt and a bit of sugar to draw out excess moisture. Let stand for 30 minutes. Place the zucchini in another colander and sprinkle with salt. Let stand for 20 minutes. Dry the zucchini well with a paper towel, then squeeze to get rid of moisture.

Preheat the oven to 350°F. Oil a 3-cup baking dish.

In a bowl, combine the tomatoes, zucchini, bread, eggs, basil, ricotta, and most of the Gruyerè and Parmesan. Season the mixture with salt and pepper. Place in the prepared pan and top evenly with the remaining cheese.

Bake until set and golden, 25 to 30 minutes. Enjoy while hot or warm.

Eggplant Variation: Preheat the oven to 400°F. Place an eggplant, weighing about 1 pound, in a baking pan. Bake, turning occasionally, until soft throughout, about 45 minutes. For a smokier taste, broil the eggplant or cook on a stove-top griddle, turning occasionally. Place the eggplant in a colander and, when cool enough to handle, remove the peel and discard the seed pockets. Chop the pulp coarsely on a cutting board and return it to the colander to drain again, 10 to 20 minutes. Transfer to a bowl and mash with a fork. There should be about ½ cup. Proceed as directed, substituting the eggplant for the drained tomatoes and chopped fresh dill or mint for the parsley. Drizzle the top with olive oil and bake as directed.

PARMESAN CHEESE PUDDING

This steamed pudding is called a *sformato* in Italy. It is cooked in a *bagno-maria* (water bath), rested, unmolded, and served with a simple sauce. In Italy, most *sformato* recipes call for puréed cooked vegetables. Because of my addiction to cheese, I like to have the vegetables as the sauce and the custard made with just cheese and eggs. To make it a vegetable *sformato*, fold in ⅓ cup puréed cooked vegetables such as broccoli or spinach with the cheese, and serve with tomato sauce. You can make this in a small glass baking dish, an individual soufflé dish, or a small loaf pan.

1 tablespoon unsalted butter

1 tablespoon all-purpose flour

½ cup half-and-half or light cream

¼ cup milk

1 whole egg plus 1 egg yolk

⅔ cup grated Parmesan cheese

Pinch of salt

Freshly ground black pepper

Freshly grated nutmeg (optional)

Preheat the oven to 350°F. Butter an individual soufflé dish or a small loaf pan, line it with baker's parchment, and butter the parchment.

In a small saucepan, melt the butter over medium heat. Add the flour and stir well, reduce the heat to low, and cook, stirring, for about 3 minutes. Add the half-and-half and whisk until thickened, about 4 minutes. Remove from the heat, stir in the milk, whole egg and egg yolk, and cheese, and season to taste with salt and pepper. Sometimes it's nice to add a grating of nutmeg. Spoon the cheese custard mixture into the prepared mold.

Place the mold in a baking pan and add hot water to the pan to reach halfway up the sides of the mold. Cover the pan with aluminum foil and bake until a knife inserted into the center of the pudding comes out clean, about 20 to 25 minutes. Remove the mold from the water bath. Let rest for 5 minutes, then run a knife around the inside edge of the mold, invert a dinner plate on top, shake once, and invert the mold and the plate together. Serve with one of the following sauces.

continued

Mushroom Sauce: Sauté 4 ounces fresh mushrooms, wiped clean and coarsely chopped, in 1½ tablespoons unsalted butter until tender. Add a little minced garlic and some chopped fresh chives or thyme, and season with salt and freshly ground black pepper.

Green Vegetable Sauce: In a blender, purée ½ cup thawed frozen English peas or cooked broccoli, zucchini, or asparagus with ¼ cup chicken stock and 1 tablespoon extra-virgin olive oil or heavy cream until smooth. Season with salt and freshly ground black pepper. Heat gently to serve.

Red Pepper Sauce: In a sauté pan, heat 3 tablespoons olive oil over medium heat. Add 1 small onion, chopped, and cook, stirring, until very soft, 12 to 15 minutes. Transfer to a food processor or blender and add 3 roasted red bell peppers, peeled, seeded, and chopped, and pulse to a coarse purée. Add lemon juice, salt, and freshly ground black pepper to taste. Beat in a little more oil and water or vegetable stock if the purée is too dense. Garnish with chopped fresh flat-leaf parsley or basil when serving.

This sauce also is good on pasta or spooned over broiled or poached fish or chicken.

QUESADILLA

This is one of my favorite comfort-food suppers, but it is also good for a Sunday lunch when I have time to curl up with the paper. I know it's all right to use canned chiles, but I like to roast a poblano chile (often mistakenly labeled pasilla), then use the leftover for another dish, ideally something with corn. Flour tortillas are traditional for quesadillas, but you can also use corn. Corn tortillas are thicker and tend to crack when folded, so place the topping on one tortilla and cover with another, cook it, and then cut later.

1 poblano chile

1 ripe avocado

2 flour tortillas

½ cup shredded Monterey Jack cheese

½ teaspoon chili powder such as Grandma's or Gebhardt

2 green onions, including tender green tops, finely chopped

2 tablespoons finely chopped fresh cilantro (optional)

Salt and freshly ground black pepper

Canola or corn oil for frying

Salsa (see Molho di Pimentão variations, page 21; optional)

Roast the chile over an open gas flame on the stove top or under the broiler until charred on all sides. Turn often and watch carefully. Do not overcook, as it will fall apart. Place the chile in a plastic bag or a covered container and let stand for 10 minutes. Peel and cut in half; remove the stem and seeds. Reserve half for another use, and cut half into ¼-inch dice or lengthwise into ⅛-inch-wide strips.

Cut the avocado in half. Reserve half for another use (see Tortilla and Lime Soup, page 39), wrapping it tightly in plastic wrap to prevent discoloration. Scoop the avocado flesh from the skin with a spoon and cut lengthwise into thin slices.

Lay the tortillas on a work surface. Distribute ¼ cup of the cheese on half of each tortilla. Sprinkle the chili powder evenly over the cheese, then top with the chile, avocado, green onions, cilantro, (if using), and a sprinkling of salt and pepper. Gently fold each filled tortilla in half. You may assemble these ahead of time and refrigerate for up to a day before cooking.

Heat a griddle or large sauté pan over low heat and brush lightly with oil. Place the tortillas on the griddle, weight slightly with a pan lid, and cook, turning once, until pale golden brown on both sides, about 5 minutes total. Slide onto a cutting board, cut in half, and transfer to a plate, Serve with salsa, if desired.

FRITTATA with POTATOES, ZUCCHINI, and RED PEPPER

Italian frittatas resemble the Spanish omelets called tortillas. They are thick and firm and are usually served at room temperature, cut into wedges. But it's hard to make one in a single portion and give it sufficient depth and texture. However, you can eat half one day and half at another time. It also may be reheated in a microwave and topped with a little Pesto (page 33) thinned with a bit of olive oil.

½ cup pure olive oil, or as needed

1 large russet potato, peeled and cut into ⅛-inch-thick slices

Salt and freshly ground black pepper

2 small zucchini, thinly sliced

2 tablespoons chopped fresh basil or ½ teaspoon dried oregano

1 small onion, thinly sliced

A few roasted red bell pepper strips

5 eggs

Grated Parmesan cheese (optional)

In a nonstick or well-seasoned sauté pan about 8 inches in diameter, heat 2 or 3 tablespoons of the olive oil over medium heat. Add the potato and cook, turning often, until tender and golden, about 10 minutes. Season with salt and pepper. Remove the potato slices with a slotted spatula and set aside in a bowl. Add 2 tablespoons oil to the same pan and fry the zucchini, turning once, until tender and slightly golden, about 4 minutes. Add the basil and season with salt and pepper. Using the slotted spatula, add the zucchini to the potatoes.

Add enough oil to the pan to total 2 tablespoons and return to medium heat. Add the onion and sauté until soft and tender, about 10 minutes. Season with salt and pepper. Remove with the slotted spatula and add to the potatoes. Add the bell pepper strips to the vegetable mixture.

In a large bowl, beat the eggs until well blended, adding a little of the Parmesan, if using. Add to the vegetables. Return the saucepan to the heat and add 2 tablespoons oil. When it is hot, pour in the egg mixture. Reduce the heat to low and cook until golden on the bottom, 8 to 10 minutes. Invert a flat platter over the pan and invert the pan and the platter together, lifting off the pan. Add 1 or 2 tablespoons oil to the pan and slide the omelet, cooked-side up, back into the pan. Cook until golden brown on the bottom, 3 or 4 minutes longer.

Slide the frittata out onto a serving platter. Let cool a bit, then cut in half and set aside half. Cut the remaining half into wedges and enjoy for dinner. Cover the other half and refrigerate for up to 2 days for another supper. Bring to room temperature before serving.

Note: If all this flipping makes you nervous, instead of sautéing the frittata, you may bake it in an oiled baking dish in a 350°F oven until the top is golden, 25 to 30 minutes.

Fish and Seafood

Fish and Shellfish

Freshness is the key when it comes to fish and shellfish. I try to shop for seafood the day I plan to eat it. Unlike meat and poultry, which can hang around for a day or two in the refrigerator without any loss of texture or flavor, seafood suffers if stored for more than a day. While I might have an idea of what I'd like to cook, the real inspiration comes the minute I look into the iced display case at my fish market and see what looks best that day. Fish and shellfish are fast and easy to cook, making them ideal candidates for evenings when I don't have a lot of time to get dinner on the table. A piece of tuna cooks in seven or eight minutes, giving me just enough time to prepare the sauce (or grab one from my pantry) and steam some broccoli. Fillet of sole cooks in six minutes, leaving enough time to squeeze lemon juice, rinse capers or toast almonds for the sauce, and wilt some spinach. Shrimp and scallops cook in only four minutes.

While fish and shellfish are typically expensive in restaurants, they are a bargain when you cook them for yourself. At my local market, certain fish are standbys: salmon, halibut, swordfish, sole, rock cod, trout, and tuna are usually available, and because they are popular, they are inevitably fresh due to constant turnover. (I try to pay attention to news reports on what fish might be temporarily in danger of being overfished, and resist buying them, no matter how delicious they are.) I love the crunch of shrimp and squid, the soft sweetness of crab, and the delicate texture of scallops, and I have a longstanding passion for lobster that goes back to my childhood. I like the briny saltiness of clams and the earthy sweetness of mussels. On certain evenings I might use an assortment of fish and shellfish to make a soup, a stew, or a fragrant curry. Seafood figures in many pastas and risottos (see the Pasta and Grains chapter), too, because a little goes a long way.

LOBSTER for ONE

The simplest and easiest way to prepare a lobster is to boil it gently for about 10 minutes and serve it with drawn or flavored butter. A two pounder is a perfect, messy dinner best eaten alone so you can dig in and crack shells, lick your fingers, and suck noisily on the little legs. When I am in an especially festive mood, I might prepare lobster in a more elaborate way, such as grilled or roasted, which results in a different texture and the meat perfumed in a different way.

Most recipes for grilled or roasted lobster require you to kill the shellfish while it is alive; however, I am too squeamish to plunge a knife into the back of a lobster's head while it is still kicking, even though I can drop it into boiling water without a qualm. So I take the coward's way out and drop it into heavily salted boiling water, cook it for 6 or 7 minutes, depending on its size, and then plunge it into an ice-water bath. (Some cooks believe that it's easier to remove the lobster meat from the shell if you haven't iced it, because the unchilled flesh doesn't adhere to the shell. But I think it's safer to chill the lobster and not worry about it spoiling.)

Once it has cooled in the ice-water bath, place the partially cooked lobster on a cutting board and, with a sharp knife or cleaver, cut it in half from top to bottom. Remove the gravelly sac at the lobster's head and the long intestinal vein that runs down the center. Save any coral or roe to add to the sauce. Detach the claws from the body, and carefully remove all claw and knuckle meat. Lobster crackers or a mallet and

continued

A Special Occasion

Years ago, I wrote a newspaper column about my favorite childhood restaurant memories. In it I mentioned Lundy's, a famous seafood restaurant in Brooklyn, where I spent many an idyllic Sunday eating steamers, lobster, biscuits, and warm huckleberry pie. I talked about how my favorite waiter applauded the day I ate my first whole lobster. After the article appeared, I received a letter from a fellow Brooklynite, now a doctor, who told me that his family, to avoid an additional lobster expense, would order lobsters for themselves and chicken for him, then eat the lobster and put his chicken in their empty lobster shells. He's still upset.

A steamed lobster with melted butter, French fries, and a glass of fine white Burgundy is my idea of heaven. While lobster is invariably an expensive restaurant item, it is a relative bargain at home. Because of its cachet, however, lobster always feels like an extravagance. To Elena, my granddaughter, it is the ideal "special occasion" dish. I make it for her on her birthday or any time we have a family celebration. The first time Elena tasted lobster she loved it and began asking for it every week. Finally my son explained to her that lobster was for special occasions, not for the everyday family dinner. Quite often when we dine together she asks, with hope in her voice, if the dinner is going to be a "special occasion."

sharp small kitchen shears or scissors work well. If you plan on grilling the lobster meat in its shell, remove the tail meat and cut it into 2-inch segments, then put it back into the shell body along with the claw and knuckle meat. If you will be roasting the lobster and the shell is not crucial to your aesthetics, put the lobster meat in a buttered or oiled gratin dish. In either case, if desired, drizzle liberal amounts of marinade (page 110) over the lobster meat and let stand for about 20 minutes at room temperature, or up to 1 hour in the refrigerator. The marinade will tenderize and perfume the lobster meat and deliver a more velvety texture.

If you wish to grill or broil the lobster in its shell but it has not been marinated, brush on all sides with flavored oil and drizzle the meat with a marinade. Alternatively, spread a compound butter (page 112) over the lobster meat. Place the lobster halves, shell-side down, on a grill rack over a charcoal fire or on a broiler pan. Tent with aluminum foil if using a charcoal grill. Grill or broil for about 5 minutes to heat through. If you have used a marinade, baste with additional marinade as it cooks.

If you wish to roast the lobster, preheat the oven to 350°F. Place the lobster meat in its shell in a baking pan or gratin dish. If not already marinated, drizzle the lobster meat with a marinade or spread with a compound butter. Roast for 10 or 12 minutes to heat through.

TWO MARINADES for GRILLED or ROASTED SHELLFISH and FISH

These marinades will keep for 2 or 3 days in the refrigerator and are great with broiled or grilled lobsters, shrimp, scallops, or fish. Marinate the shellfish for no longer than 20 minutes at room temperature or up to 1 hour in the refrigerator. Reserve some of the marinade for basting during cooking. The same marinades are delicious with chicken as well, which can marinate as long as overnight in the refrigerator.

Mexican Citrus and Chile Marinade

MAKES ABOUT ½ CUP

2 tablespoons olive oil

2 tablespoons fresh lime juice

3 tablespoons fresh orange juice

1 teaspoon finely minced garlic

½ teaspoon finely minced jalapeño chile, or to taste

1 teaspoon grated orange zest

½ teaspoon grated lime zest

1 teaspoon ancho chile powder

⅛ teaspoon ground allspice or cinnamon

Pinch of cayenne pepper, or to taste

Salt and freshly ground black pepper

Serve the marinated and cooked shellfish or fish with black beans, warm tortillas, Molho di Pimentão (page 21) enhanced with tomatoes and onion to make a salsa, and a lime wedge, or with fried potatoes and with diced avocado tossed with the *molho*.

In a small bowl, combine all the ingredients, including salt and black pepper to taste, and whisk together lightly.

Moroccan Charmoula Marinade

Serve the marinated and cooked shellfish or fish with couscous or spicy fried potatoes, or green beans with cumin and lemon zest. This marinade is also good spooned over broiled or poached fish or used as a marinade for chicken or lamb chops. It can be thinned with olive oil and lemon juice, turning it into a dynamite vinaigrette for grilled vegetables or a tuna and bean salad.

In a small bowl, whisk together the spices, garlic, lemon juice, parsley, cilantro, and the preserved lemon, if using. Whisk in enough olive oil to make a thick, but fluid, sauce. Season to taste with salt and pepper.

MAKES ABOUT ½ CUP

1 teaspoon sweet paprika or *pimentón de la Vera* (page 22)

Pinch of cayenne pepper

½ teaspoon ground cumin

⅛ teaspoon ground ginger

Pinch of ground turmeric

2 cloves garlic, finely minced

2 tablespoons fresh lemon juice

2 tablespoons chopped fresh flat-leaf parsley

2 tablespoons chopped fresh cilantro

1 tablespoon chopped preserved lemon (optional)

¼ cup pure olive oil, or as needed

Salt and freshly ground black pepper

THREE COMPOUND BUTTERS for SHELLFISH and FISH

Spread these butters over fish or shellfish before roasting, broiling, or grilling. They are especially good on lobster, fish steaks, shrimp, and scallops. If you like, you can make a double batch and store half in the freezer for up to 2 months.

Pesto Butter

Combine 4 tablespoons (½ stick) unsalted butter at room temperature with ¼ cup Pesto (page 33). Season to taste with salt and freshly ground black pepper and maybe 1 tablespoon fresh lemon juice. Serve the seafood with fried potatoes and green beans.

Tandoori Butter

Combine 4 tablespoons (½ stick) unsalted butter at room temperature with 1 tablespoon grated fresh ginger, 1 teaspoon finely minced garlic, 1 tablespoon ground coriander, ½ teaspoon ground turmeric, ¼ teaspoon cayenne pepper, and 2 teaspoons fresh lemon juice. Season with salt and freshly ground black pepper. Serve the seafood with saffron rice and green beans or spinach.

Ginger-Shallot Butter

Melt 1 tablespoon unsalted butter in a saucepan. Add 2 tablespoons minced shallot and cook gently for a few minutes. Add 2 tablespoons dry white vermouth or white wine and simmer until the liquid is absorbed and the shallot is tender, about 2 minutes longer. Let cool to room temperature. When cool, add 1 tablespoon peeled and grated fresh ginger, 1 teaspoon chopped fresh chives, and 3 tablespoons unsalted butter at room temperature, and mix well to combine. Serve the seafood with steamed rice and green beans, asparagus, or spinach.

BAKED HALIBUT with TOMATOES and BREAD CRUMBS

Northern halibut, from cold Alaskan waters, has the most incredible buttery texture, falling into large flakes after cooking. (My local California halibut is a leaner fish and has a tendency to dry out quickly.) While I often broil it and serve it with butter-enriched Indonesian Sweet Soy Sauce (page 32) or with Moroccan Charmoula Marinade (page 111), here's a great way to bake it using some of the ingredients in your pantry. Cinnamon and oregano will give it a bit of a Greek accent.

1 halibut fillet, about 8 ounces and ¾ to 1 inch thick

1 tablespoon olive oil, plus more for drizzling

2 teaspoons fresh lemon juice

Salt and freshly ground black pepper

½ cup peeled, seeded, and chopped tomatoes

1 clove garlic, finely minced

¼ cup dry white wine

2 tablespoons chopped fresh flat-leaf parsley

Pinch of dried oregano and/or cinnamon (optional)

¼ cup dried bread crumbs or Toasted Bread Crumbs (page 82)

In a baking dish, marinate the fish in the 1 tablespoon olive oil, the lemon juice, and salt and pepper to taste for 30 minutes.

Meanwhile, in a saucepan, combine the tomatoes, garlic, wine, parsley, and the oregano and/or cinnamon, if using. Place over medium heat, bring to a simmer, reduce the heat to low, and cook for about 10 minutes to blend flavors. Season with salt and pepper. Remove from the heat.

Preheat the oven to 400°F. Pour the tomato sauce over the fish and top evenly with the bread crumbs. Drizzle with olive oil. Bake until the fish tests done (it should appear opaque when pierced with the point of a knife) and the bread crumbs are golden brown, about 15 minutes. Eat while piping hot.

POACHED SALMON with MUSHROOMS, TARRAGON, and CREAM

2 tablespoons unsalted butter

4 ounces fresh mushrooms, wiped clean and sliced

Salt and freshly ground black pepper

1 1/2 cups dry white wine, dry white vermouth, or part wine and part water

1 salmon fillet, about 6 ounces, skinned

1/3 cup heavy cream

1 tablespoon chopped fresh tarragon, plus more for garnish

Because salmon is so easy to cook at home, I almost never order it in restaurants. I can poach it in white or red wine and make a sauce by adding some cream to the pan. I can thin Peppery Prune Sauce (page 24) with some of the wine and spoon it over the poached fish. I can also broil salmon and drizzle it with Indonesian Soy Sauce (page 32) or Pesto (page 33). When I want an elegant salmon supper, however, this is the recipe I return to over and over again. It combines three of my favorite ingredients, fresh tarragon, sautéed mushrooms, and salmon. If I don't have an open bottle of white wine on hand, I use dry white vermouth, which is shelf stable.

In a small skillet, melt the butter over high heat. Add the mushrooms and sauté until they give off some liquid, about 5 minutes. Remove from the heat and season to taste with salt and pepper.

Pour the wine into a saucepan large enough to hold the salmon and bring to a simmer. Slip in the salmon, cover the pan, and poach gently over low heat until the salmon tests done (it should appear opaque when pierced with the point of a knife), 8 to 10 minutes. Remove the salmon from the poaching liquid with a slotted skimmer and set aside on a warmed plate; keep warm.

Add the cream and 1 tablespoon tarragon to the poaching liquid and reduce over high heat to a slightly syrupy sauce. Add the mushrooms and warm through. Spoon the sauce over the salmon. Garnish with a bit more tarragon.

SEAFOOD CURRY with COCONUT, CITRUS, and CUCUMBER

India and Southeast Asia provide the inspiration for the fragrant spice mixture in my all-purpose curry. Add about 8 ounces fish fillet, cut into cubes, or a mixture of fish and shellfish, about 8 ounces in all (not counting shells), to the simmering base, along with a few slices of cucumber or some blanched green beans. Serve with steamed jasmine or basmati rice and your favorite chutney.

2 tablespoons canola or corn oil

½ onion, chopped

2 teaspoons each finely minced garlic and grated fresh ginger

1 teaspoon grated lime or lemon zest

1 teaspoon each ground coriander and cumin toasted in a dry pan

½ teaspoon ground black pepper, toasted in a dry pan

1 teaspoon minced jalapeño chile, or to taste

½ cup canned coconut milk

1 cup fish or chicken stock

1 tablespoon fresh lime juice, or to taste

1 tablespoon brown sugar, or to taste

Salt

½ small cucumber, peeled, quartered lengthwise, seeded, and cut into 2-inch pieces

6 ounces firm white fish fillet, cut into 2-inch cubes

4 medium or large shrimp, peeled and deveined

4 scallops, muscles removed

8 clams, well scrubbed (optional)

1 tablespoon chopped fresh mint

2 tablespoons chopped fresh cilantro or Thai basil

In a very large saucepan or wide sauté pan, heat the oil over medium heat. Add the onion and cook until tender and translucent, 5 to 8 minutes. Add the garlic, ginger, lime zest, coriander, cumin, pepper, and chile and cook for 3 minutes longer. Add the coconut milk, stock, lime juice, brown sugar, and salt to taste and bring to a boil. Reduce the heat immediately and simmer for 5 minutes to blend the flavors. This is the curry base. It can be made a day ahead, covered, and refrigerated.

Bring a saucepan of salted water to a boil, add the cucumber, and parboil for 2 minutes. Drain and refresh in cold water. Drain again and set aside.

Ten minutes before serving, in a saucepan, bring the curry base to a simmer. Add the cubed fish and cook until the fish is tender and cooked through but not falling apart, 5 to 8 minutes, adding the shellfish and cucumber during the last 3 to 5 minutes. Spoon into a serving dish and garnish with the mint and the cilantro.

Variation: You can easily transform this seafood curry into a chicken curry by adding 8 ounces boneless chicken, cut into 1-inch cubes, in place of the fish and shellfish, and using chicken stock instead of fish stock. Sliced zucchini or green beans may be added instead of the cucumber.

SOLE PICCATA

In the frenetic quest for originality and novelty that seems to drive many food publications and restaurant menus, scores of good dishes fall by the wayside. I'd like to bring this oldie but goodie back. One of the quickest and probably most popular ways to prepare sole is with butter and lemon, but I love it in the Italian style called piccata, with lemon and capers. Serve with roasted or steamed potatoes and spinach or broccoli. This recipe also works well with trout.

¼ cup all-purpose flour

Salt and freshly ground black pepper

8 ounces Dover or petrale sole fillet

4 tablespoons (½ stick) unsalted butter

1 tablespoon fresh lemon juice

1 tablespoon capers, rinsed

Chopped fresh flat-leaf parsley for garnish

Spread the flour on a plate and season with salt and pepper. Dredge the fish fillet in the seasoned flour, tapping off the excess.

In a large sauté pan, heat 3 tablespoons of the butter over medium-high heat. Add the fish fillet and sauté quickly, turning once, until it is golden brown on both sides, about 4 to 6 minutes total. With a slotted spatula, remove the fish to a warmed dinner plate.

Add the lemon juice and capers to the pan juices over low heat. Stir in the remaining 1 tablespoon butter for a thicker sauce. Pour over the fish and top with the parsley.

Variations: You can also break up the cooked fish, return it to the caper and lemon sauce, and toss with cooked linguine.

Sole amandine is another simple and delicious old-fashioned dish. To make it, omit the capers and fry a few tablespoons of slivered blanched almonds in the pan juices until bubbly and golden. Spoon the almonds and juices over the fish.

SWORDFISH in a SICILIAN SAUCE

Sometimes this is called *pesce spada alla ghiotta*, sometimes *alla stemperata*. Regardless of the name, it's that offbeat Sicilian combo of garlic, pine nuts, raisins, capers, and olives, sometimes combined with tomatoes, and sometimes not, that seduces me every time.

¼ cup all-purpose flour

Salt and freshly ground black pepper

1 swordfish fillet, about 8 ounces and 1 inch thick

About 3 tablespoons extra-virgin olive oil

½ small onion, chopped

1 celery stalk, chopped

½ cup peeled, seeded, and chopped tomatoes (optional)

2 tablespoons green olives, pitted and coarsely chopped

2 tablespoons pine nuts, toasted

2 tablespoons raisins, plumped in hot water

1 tablespoon capers, rinsed

1 clove garlic, finely minced

¼ cup fish stock, dry white wine, or water

Preheat the oven to 400°F. Lightly oil a baking dish that will accommodate the fish fillet. On a flat plate, stir together the flour with a little salt and pepper, then dredge the fish in the seasoned flour and shake off the excess.

In a sauté pan, heat about 1 tablespoon oil, or as needed to form a film in the pan, over medium-high heat. Sauté the fish on both sides until lightly colored. With a slotted spatula, remove the fish to the prepared baking dish.

In the same sauté pan, heat 2 tablespoons olive oil over medium heat. Add the onion and celery and sauté until soft and pale gold, about 10 minutes. Add the tomatoes, if using, and simmer for 3 minutes to thicken slightly. Add the olives, pine nuts, raisins, capers, garlic, and stock, and simmer for 8 to 10 minutes to blend the flavors. Taste and adjust the seasoning.

Ladle the sauce over the fish. Bake until the fish tests done with the point of a knife, about 10 minutes. Eat while hot or warm.

Variation: You can also make this dish in a sauté pan. Just place the sautéed fish in the sauce in the pan, cover, and simmer gently over low heat until the fish is cooked through, about 10 minutes.

TUNA STEAK TWO WAYS

Here are two of my favorite ways to prepare a tuna steak at home. You can use the less-expensive albacore if you don't want to spring for ahi. It may not have the meaty red color, but it will still taste good.

Tuna in a Black Pepper Crust with Lemon Butter

Here is steak au poivre made with tuna. Sautéed spinach and fried potatoes are ideal accompaniments.

2 tablespoons unsalted butter at room temperature

1 teaspoon grated lemon zest and 2 teaspoons fresh lemon juice, or to taste

Salt

1 tuna steak, 6 or 7 ounces and about 1 inch thick

3 tablespoons olive oil

1 tablespoon freshly cracked (not too fine, not too coarse) black pepper

To make the lemon butter, in a small bowl, combine the butter with the zest and juice and the salt to taste. Set aside.

Coat the tuna with 1 tablespoon of the olive oil, then dip in the cracked pepper. Sprinkle with salt.

Heat the remaining 2 tablespoons olive oil in a cast-iron pan or a heavy nonstick pan over high heat. Add the tuna and sauté for about 3 minutes on each side. It should be crusty on the outside and medium-rare in the center. (You may cook it longer if you prefer it more well done.) Transfer to a warmed place and top with the lemon butter. Eat at once.

Variations: Tuna is versatile. A simple steak or fillet broiled, grilled, or sautéed without a crust can be topped with a spoonful of Pesto (page 33). Also try the Moroccan Charmoula Marinade (page 111), one of the compound butters (page 112), or Indonesian Sweet Soy Sauce (page 32).

Tuna in a Fennel-Bread Crumb Crust

The tuna should be cut about an inch thick to prevent it from drying out while cooking. Use a cast-iron pan or heavy nonstick pan as it helps the crust to brown and set up quickly. The dish is a bit austere, so I often add a dollop of aioli flavored with red pepper as a sauce. It seems to make the dish more elegant. Or you may sauce it with a *raita* of yogurt flavored with chopped cucumber, tomatoes, and garlic. Accompany with sautéed chard or spinach.

1 tuna steak, 6 or 7 ounces and about 1 inch thick

3 tablespoons olive oil

1 teaspoon fresh lemon juice

Salt and freshly ground black pepper

5 tablespoons dried bread crumbs

1 tablespoon ground fennel or cumin, toasted in a dry pan

Red Pepper Aioli (page 35)

In a shallow dish, marinate the tuna in 1 tablespoon of the olive oil and the lemon juice for a few hours in the refrigerator. If you are short of time, you may cut this to 10 to 15 minutes at room temperature.

Just before cooking, sprinkle the fish with salt and pepper. In another shallow dish, stir together the bread crumbs and the fennel. Dredge the tuna in the bread crumb mixture.

Heat the remaining 2 tablespoons olive oil in a cast-iron pan or a heavy nonstick pan over high heat. Add the tuna and sauté for about 3 minutes on each side. It should be crusty and light brown on the outside and medium-rare in the center. (You may cook it longer, if you prefer it more well done.) Transfer to a warmed plate, top with the aioli, and eat hot.

Variation: For a citrus flavor, add a little grated orange zest to the bread crumb mixture and a squeeze of orange juice to the oil in which the fish is marinated. Serve with a butter seasoned with lemon or orange zest, in place of the aioli. You may also grill or broil the fish rather than sauté it. This method works with salmon.

MeAt

Poultry and **Meat**

Poultry and Meat

While vegetables and grains are always an essential part of my diet, I choose to eat meat and/or poultry a few times a week. They are economical with my time and my budget, and they can be purchased a few days in advance of the meal without fear of spoilage. Also, with one meal I can prepare enough for leftovers and creative recycles.

I always prefer the taste and texture of poultry cooked on the bone. But boneless cuts have their usefulness, especially when time and ease are considerations. Roasting a whole chicken takes more than an hour, while a boneless chicken breast can be sautéed in ten minutes. Boneless chicken can be diced and tossed with pasta or risotto, poached in soup, or skewered and broiled. I prefer using dark meat for most boneless chicken preparations, as it is moister and delivers more taste.

Although my favorite cut of lamb is the leg, I will not roast a whole leg just for me. Leg of lamb is lean and doesn't reheat well, so I save it for family and company occasions. For solo suppers, I rely on lamb steaks cut from the leg, or loin or rib chops. As for pork, I find most chops and roasts too dry because now pigs are raised to be lean, with little of the marbling that provides moisture. The ideal cut for me is the tenderloin, which cooks quickly and remains moist. Again, I save large pork roasts for company, as they tend to dry out when reheated.

For beef suppers, I prefer rib-eye steaks, hanger steaks, and skirt steaks. I am not crazy about hamburgers on a bun, but I like them served on the plate with an appropriate sauce. Brisket, rib roast, and other large cuts are reserved for company dinners. Veal is ideal for a quick supper if it is cut into scallopini and sautéed or if it is a rib or loin chop and broiled.

I have selected some of my old standbys, from Calves' Liver with Onion and Sage to Balsamic Vinegar–Marinated Skirt Steak, so that they might become part of your solo supper repertoire.

ROAST CHICKEN with GARLIC, LEMON, and HERBS

I know that boneless, skinless chicken breasts are the answer to the question of what a solo cook should prepare for dinner. After all, they are fast, easy, and come in individual portions. But they are not my first choice when I have a craving for chicken. Nothing pleases me more than a succulent whole roasted bird. It is juicier, tastier, and comes with crackly skin. The payoff is that I will have glorious leftovers for another meal and maybe even two. And the smells in the house are worth the wait. I try to find a kosher chicken because they have been brined and are especially tasty. If my market is out of them, I buy a local free-range bird and rub it with salt and lemon. If I have time, I might put it in a brine solution, but more often than not, I pick one up and get cooking with little preparation.

1 roasting chicken, about 3½ to 4 pounds

1 juicy lemon, quartered

Kosher salt and freshly ground black pepper

4 cloves garlic, 2 crushed and 2 minced

2 teaspoons dried oregano or chopped fresh rosemary or tarragon

¼ cup pure olive oil

2 tablespoons fresh lemon juice

1 teaspoon salt

½ teaspoon coarsely cracked black pepper

Preheat the oven to 400°F.

Rinse the chicken and pat dry. Rub the bird inside and out with the lemon quarters, kosher salt, and ground pepper. (Omit the salt if the chicken has been brined.) Place the lemon quarters, 2 crushed garlic cloves, and 1 teaspoon of the oregano inside the cavity.

To prepare the basting mixture, in a small saucepan, combine the olive oil, lemon juice, the remaining 1 teaspoon oregano, the minced garlic, 1 teaspoon salt and the cracked pepper. Bring to a simmer over low heat and simmer for 3 minutes, then remove from the heat.

continued

Brush the chicken with some of the basting mixture. Place, breast-side up, on a rack in a roasting pan. Roast, basting occasionally with the olive oil mixture, until the skin is crisp and the juices run clear when the leg is pierced with a skewer, about 1¼ hours. (Some cooks recommend starting the chicken on its side, turning it after 20 minutes to the other side, and finally turning it breast-up for the last 20 minutes for more even browning.)

Remove the chicken to a carving board. Let rest for 5 to 10 minutes, then carve, drizzling the pieces with the pan juices if you like.

Suggestions for Leftovers: Add to Tortilla and Lime Soup (page 39), chicken noodle soup, Chicken and Bread Soup (page 42), risotto, or a salad. And don't forget a chicken sandwich with good mayonnaise or Aioli (page 34), sliced tomato, and lettuce.

Variety is Not Always the Spice of Life

Years ago, people did not rely on shelves of cookbooks and food magazines for inspiration. They did not dine in diverse restaurants many nights a week. Simplicity, routine, and familiarity were the norm. There was a recipe-card file or book with clippings and maybe a dog-eared cookbook or two. Certain recipes in the family's repertoire were prepared with great regularity: roast chicken on Sunday, fish on Friday, turkey with chestnut stuffing at Thanksgiving, and barbecued ribs on the Fourth of July. Every once in a while a new dish was attempted, critiqued, and added to the roster if everyone liked it. But most people were generally content to eat familiar foods prepared in recognized and traditional ways. At restaurants, the dishes on the menu were understood from their names. No waiter had to stand by and explain each dish.

Times have changed. We now have a diversity of cookbooks and restaurants that can make your head and tummy spin. We have become accustomed to the idea of trends and constant change and have been programmed to accept novelty as a way to keep boredom at bay. So, after we have prepared the same recipe a few times in a row, we feel that we are in a rut and not being creative. But, frankly, is familiarity so wrong? What if the only way you like sole is with lemon and almonds? Why not make it that way guilt free anytime you crave it? There is no need to invent a new dish every time you step into the kitchen, unless you are bored with what you are doing or want to test your creative powers. Constant stimulation and change can be unsettling and unnecessary. In fact, familiar recipes are a good thing when we cook at home. If we need new ideas, we can dine out, try a new dish, and if we like it, go home and replicate what we ate. We can choose to experiment from time to time. However, if we revert to our old favorites with regularity, it's perfectly okay. That's the essence of home cooking.

CHICKEN with PANCETTA and SUN-DRIED TOMATOES

Every now and again, I break down and buy boneless chicken breasts or thighs, rather than a whole bird. This quick sauté is delicious with mashed or roasted potatoes, or resting atop soft polenta. Broccoli or green beans are also good accompaniments. You also can turn the sauté into a sauce for fusilli or rigatoni by tossing it with the cooked pasta.

I always have sliced pancetta on hand in the freezer and sun-dried tomatoes in my pantry. When sun-dried tomatoes were introduced to the American marketplace, they appeared on every restaurant menu and in every cooking publication. The overkill made me not want to eat them. To appreciate them anew, I ignored them for a few years; now I use them when I think they are essential. They make this dish delicious.

2 ounces pancetta, sliced ¼ inch thick, then uncoiled and cut cross-wise into ¼-inch-wide strips

3 tablespoons olive oil (or part oil from the sun-dried tomatoes)

1 whole chicken breast, boned, skinned, and cut into 2-inch chunks

Salt and freshly ground black pepper

½ cup sliced red onion (¼ inch thick)

2 tablespoons oil-packed sun-dried tomatoes, cut into narrow strips

2 teaspoons finely minced garlic

⅓ cup chicken stock

2 tablespoons chopped fresh basil

2 tablespoons niçoise olives (optional)

In a sauté pan, render the pancetta in 1 teaspoon of the olive oil over medium heat until it is half-cooked. It will reduce in volume to about 2 tablespoons. With a slotted spoon, remove the pancetta to a plate.

Sprinkle the chicken pieces with salt and pepper. Add 2 tablespoons of the oil to the fat remaining in the pan over high heat. Add the chicken pieces and brown on both sides. Remove from the pan with a slotted spoon to a separate plate. Discard the oil from the sauté pan.

Add the remaining 2 teaspoons oil to the same pan over medium heat. Add the onion and cook until pale gold, about 10 minutes. Stir in the pancetta, sun dried-tomatoes, and garlic and cook for 2 minutes. Add the chicken stock, allow it to reduce a bit, and then return the chicken pieces along with half of the basil to the pan and heat through. Transfer to a warmed plate and garnish with remaining basil and the olives, if using.

SALTIMBOCCA alla ROMANA

Saltimbocca, veal sautéed with prosciutto and sage, is a festive and easy supper. A classic of Roman cuisine, saltimbocca means "jumps in the mouth." Although veal scallops are traditional, the dish also can be prepared with boneless slices of turkey breast or boneless chicken breasts. Some cooks don't like the prosciutto side to get crispy, but this doesn't bother me. The pan may be deglazed with stock alone or in combination with wine. I like to serve saltimbocca with green beans or spinach, and mashed potatoes are nice if you want a starch accompaniment.

2 large veal scallops or uncooked boneless turkey breast slices, about 8 to 10 ounces total weight and each 1/3 inch thick, or 2 boneless, skinless chicken breast halves

Salt and freshly ground black pepper

4 fresh sage leaves

2 thin slices prosciutto

1 1/2 tablespoons olive oil

1/2 cup chicken stock reduced to 1/4 cup

1/4 cup dry Marsala, dry white wine, or additional stock

1 tablespoon unsalted butter

Pound the meat lightly between sheets of plastic wrap to a uniform thickness of 1/4 inch. Sprinkle lightly with salt and pepper and top each piece with 2 sage leaves. Cover the sage with the prosciutto slices and skewer in place with toothpicks.

In a sauté pan, heat the oil over medium-high heat. Add the meat, prosciutto-and-sage-side down, and sauté until golden on the first side, about 3 minutes. Turn and cook the other side until golden, about 3 minutes longer. Remove to a warmed plate and keep warm.

Pour in the stock and the wine and deglaze the pan over high heat, scraping up any brown bits stuck to the bottom. Boil until the pan juices reduce and are thickened. Remove the pan from the heat and swirl in the butter. Spoon over the saltimbocca and eat at once.

ROAST DUCK with LEMON and ROSEMARY

1 Pekin or Long Island duck, about 5 pounds

2 teaspoons kosher salt

1 teaspoon freshly ground black pepper

½ teaspoon freshly grated nutmeg

1 teaspoon minced garlic

2 teaspoons grated lemon zest

2 teaspoons chopped fresh rosemary

½ cup dry white wine

I know it's not the most practical dinner for one, but I occasionally get a craving for roast duck. Why? Nostalgia. When I was a little girl, my father would drive us out to a remote (or at least it seemed that way to me) part of Long Island to a lakeside restaurant called Villa Victor, which specialized in roast duckling. The trip was an adventure to the "countryside," away from the concrete of our Brooklyn streets. My craving, however, creates the dilemma of what to do with the leftover half duck. I know it will not be quite as crisp and crackling as the first time, but it can be reheated easily. Simply refrigerate it, then bring it back to room temperature the next day. Arrange the pieces, skin-side down, in a cast-iron or other heavy skillet. Place in a very hot oven, 450 to 500° F, until sizzling and crispy, 7 to 10 minutes. Or use the cooked duck meat in a salad (page 65). Serve the roast duck with sautéed pear or apple slices.

Rinse the duck and pat dry. Cut off the wing tips, the neck, and feet. Trim any excess fat from inside the cavity. In a small bowl, stir together the kosher salt, pepper, nutmeg, garlic, lemon zest, and rosemary and rub the mixture all over the bird, inside and out. Cover and refrigerate overnight if you have the time.

Preheat the oven to 450°F. Prick the duck skin with the tines of a fork in the fattiest areas (the thighs and breast), to allow some fat to drain away while roasting. Place the duck, breast-side up, on a rack in a roasting pan and roast until the skin is golden and crisp, about 1 hour. The meat will be moist and juicy, and the juices will run clear when the thigh joint is pierced.

Personal **Celebrations**

Foods that I cook for personal celebrations, are, in essence, simple dishes, but require some finesse and skill if they are to attain the level of perfection that they inherently promise. They may remind me of a happy time or place. They may promote comfort that comes from familiarity, or the excitement of eating something only rarely enjoyed at home alone.

So it might be a lobster, roast duck, or two dozen oysters and a Caesar salad. I realize that some dishes I've selected for my private parties at home might be considered very rich, not exactly health food; but they do fall into the old traditional Mediterranean pattern of fasting and feasting. I eat these to feast. And while I don't fast very much, I am a relatively sensible eater most of the time—a grown-up at last.

Remove the duck from the oven, transfer to a cutting board, and let rest for 5 to 10 minutes. Meanwhile, spoon off the fat from pan and place the pan on the stove top over medium-high heat. Add the wine and deglaze the pan, scraping up any browned bits from the bottom. Carve the duck into quarters. Pour the pan juices over the half duck that you are eating now. Set aside half of the duck for another meal (see recipe introduction).

Note: If you are roasting the duck at 450ºF, plan for about 12 minutes per pound. For more meltingly tender meat, preheat the oven to 350ºF and roast for about 20 minutes per pound. The skin will be not quite as crisp, but the meat will be much softer.

KABOB with PEANUT SAUCE

Kabobs are an easy and satisfying dinner for one. The meat can be cubed ahead of time, even the day before, and marinated at room temperature for 1 hour or longer in the refrigerator. The kabobs can instead be served with a fruit-based salsa or Sun Gold Tomato Chutney (page 30). This recipe can be doubled easily, and it works for firm white fish fillets as well.

MARINADE

1 plump clove garlic, chopped

1-inch piece fresh ginger, peeled and sliced

1 tablespoon minced green onion, including tender green tops

1 teaspoon grated lemon zest or 1 tablespoon minced lemongrass

1 tablespoon soy sauce

1 tablespoon bourbon, white wine, or sherry

1 teaspoon Asian sesame oil

1/2 teaspoon freshly ground white pepper

2 or 3 boneless, skinless chicken thighs; 1 beef fillet, about 8 to 10 ounces; 8 to 10 ounces pork tender-loin; or 1 lamb steak, about 8 to 10 ounces and 1 inch thick, boned

Olive or peanut oil

Salt and freshly ground black pepper

1/3 cup Peanut Sauce (page 27)

To make the marinade: Combine the garlic, ginger, green onion, and lemon zest in the container of a mini-processor or blender. Pulse to purée. Add the soy, bourbon, sesame oil, and pepper and blend briefly. You can make this marinade the day before you use it.

Cut the poultry into 1-inch cubes and place in a shallow nonreactive dish. Pour the marinade on top and toss to coat evenly. Cover and marinate for 1 hour at room temperature or 2 to 4 hours in the refrigerator, turning the meat occasionally.

Preheat the broiler or prepare a fire in the charcoal grill.

Thread the poultry cubes onto a bamboo skewer that has been soaked in water for 15 minutes or onto a metal skewer. Brush with oil and sprinkle with salt and pepper. Slip under the broiler or place on the grill and cook, turning once, for 3 minutes on each side for chicken, lamb, or beef and 4 to 5 minutes on each side for pork. The kabob should be nicely browned but still juicy. Serve with the Peanut Sauce.

SAUTÉED DUCK BREAST

A sautéed duck breast may not be quite as festive as roast duck cooked on the bone, but it makes a great solo supper—as good and as simple to prepare as a steak. Sear it to brown crispiness, then finish in the oven or in the pan over low heat. Make a plain pan sauce or use one of the pantry sauces you have on hand. Stores like Trader Joe's have Muscovy duck breasts in the freezer case, and good butcher and poultry shops carry them, too.

Boneless Muscovy duck breast half, about 12 ounces

Salt and freshly ground black pepper

Pinch of ground cinnamon, allspice, or five-spice powder (optional)

½ cup chicken stock or dry red wine

About 3 tablespoons Peppery Prune Sauce (page 24), or Pomegranate Marinade and Basting Sauce (page 26) (optional)

Preheat the oven to 450°F. Rinse the duck breast and pat dry. Using a sharp knife, score the skin in a crosshatch pattern, but do not cut down into the meat. Rub the duck with salt and pepper and with a bit of cinnamon, if using.

Heat a large, ovenproof sauté pan over medium heat. Place the duck breast, skin-side down, in the hot pan. Cook until the breast renders its fat, about 8 minutes. Drain off the fat from the pan and slip it into the oven for about 8 minutes for medium-rare. (You may also finish the breast on top of the stove, turning it once and sautéing for 5 to 8 minutes.) Transfer the duck breast to a cutting board and keep warm.

Return the pan to medium-high heat, add the stock and deglaze the pan, scraping up the browned bits on the pan bottom. Reduce a bit, then, if desired, spoon in one of the sauces, mix well, and heat through.

Slice the duck breast on the diagonal and arrange on a warmed plate. Spoon the pan juices over the top.

Note: A Muscovy duck breast half is filling and you may not be able to eat all of it. You can slice the leftovers and serve them in a salad. Because it is rich, it pairs well with bitter greens such as arugula, Belgian endive, and radicchio. Add some pear slices, orange segments, and thin fennel slices and toss with a vinaigrette made with orange or lemon juice, olive oil, and balsamic vinegar. See Main Dish Salads for other recipe suggestions.

TUSCAN-STYLE RIB-EYE STEAK with ROSEMARY, GARLIC, and PEPPER

Although I have been a California girl for a long time, exposed to hippie culture, brown rice, and tofu, you can't take the carnivorous New Yorker out of me. Some of my most beloved childhood food memories revolve around eating steak at New York's famous steakhouse, Peter Luger. And because I lived in Italy during my formative culinary years, it's not surprising that some of my steak recipes have an Italian accent. Steak, along with a glass of good red wine, is a sybaritic supper that gives me great energy and ever greater joy. It's hard to find a sirloin or New York cut that has great beef flavor, so I cook a rib eye with ample marbling or a hanger steak. "Pan broiling" a steak on a ridged, stove-top cast-iron griddle or searing it in a cast-iron skillet takes just minutes, almost the same time it takes to wilt some spinach in a sauté pan and open a bottle of wine. If I need a more substantial supper, I might fry or bake a potato. But if it's summer, it's more than likely that I'll have sliced tomatoes in honor of Peter Luger.

1 teaspoon finely chopped fresh rosemary

1 teaspoon finely minced garlic

½ teaspoon coarsely ground black pepper

About 1 tablespoon olive oil

1 aged rib-eye steak with ample marbling, 8 to 10 ounces

Kosher salt

Lemon wedge

In a small bowl, combine the rosemary, garlic, and pepper with enough olive oil to make a thick paste. Rub this paste onto the meat, cover, and let marinate for at least 1 hour at room temperature or for up to 8 hours in the refrigerator. Bring the meat to room temperature for cooking.

Just before cooking, sprinkle the meat with kosher salt. Heat a ridged, stove-top griddle or a cast-iron skillet over high heat. Pan broil or pan sear the steak over high heat, turning once, to desired doneness. For me, that means rare and takes about 3 minutes per side. Accompany with a lemon wedge as they do in Florence.

BALSAMIC VINEGAR–MARINATED SKIRT STEAK

Skirt steak is an underappreciated cut. It is full of beef flavor and is sufficiently tender when sliced with the grain. (Flank steak is another worthy cut for this recipe, but I find that skirt steak has better flavor and more marbling.) It usually is sold all rolled up and often weighs a pound or more. Part of it is thick, part thin. The leftovers, however, are good served at room temperature, alone, or as part of a salad (page 66). If you can find a hanger steak at your butcher, it also will work well for this recipe. Pair the steak with mashed potatoes.

1 skirt steak, about 1 pound, preferably ½ inch thick

About 3 ½ tablespoons olive oil

About 1 ½ tablespoons balsamic vinegar

¾ teaspoon freshly ground black pepper

1 large red onion, cut in ¼-inch-thick slices

1 red bell pepper (optional)

Kosher salt

Place the steak in a heavy-duty zippered plastic bag or shallow glass baking dish. Add 2 tablespoons of the olive oil, 1 tablespoon of the balsamic vinegar, and ½ teaspoon of the black pepper and turn as needed to coat evenly. Seal closed and let stand for about 2 hours at room temperature.

In a sauté pan, heat 1 tablespoon of the olive oil over medium-high heat. Add the onion and sauté until it caramelizes. This may take 15 to 20 minutes. Set aside.

Preheat the broiler or prepare a fire in the charcoal grill.

If you like roasted peppers, hold the bell pepper over the flame on a gas stove, slip it under the broiler, or place it on the grill and roast, turning as needed until the skin is well charred on all sides. Place the pepper in a plastic bag or covered container and allow it to rest for about 15 minutes. Peel off the skin and remove the stem and seeds. Cut length-wise into strips ½ inch wide. Add the bell pepper strips to the caramelized onion.

Sprinkle the steak with kosher salt. Broil or grill, turning once, for about 3 minutes on each side for rare or to desired doneness. Remove the steak to a cutting board, let rest for a few minutes, then slice across the grain as much of it as you plan to eat. Cover and refrigerate the remainder to use for a salad.

Warm the onion and bell pepper in the sauté pan with a bit more olive oil, add 1 or 2 teaspoons balsamic vinegar, the remaining 1/4 teaspoon pepper, and salt to taste. Arrange the sliced steak on a warmed plate and spoon the onion–bell pepper mixture over the top.

Note: You can also cook the steak on the stove top. Heat a cast-iron skillet or ridged, stove-top griddle pan over high heat, then cook the steak, turning once, to the desired degree of doneness. If you have used a skillet, you can deglaze the pan with a little of balsamic vinegar and then add the onion–bell pepper mixture.

RUSSIAN HAMBURGER with STROGANOFF MUSHROOMS

I am not an aficionado of fast-food hamburgers, but this Russian-inspired recipe makes me want to eat a burger because it becomes dinner. There's no roll, no ketchup—just rich sour cream–smothered mushrooms and maybe some rice or kasha on the side.

6 to 8 ounces ground beef, not too lean

2 to 3 tablespoons grated yellow onion

1 tablespoon chopped fresh dill

½ teaspoon salt, plus more to taste

¼ teaspoon freshly ground black pepper, plus more to taste

4 tablespoons (½ stick) unsalted butter

1 red onion, sliced

1 teaspoon paprika

8 ounces fresh mushrooms, wiped clean and sliced

¼ cup beef stock

¼ cup sour cream at room temperature

In a bowl, combine the ground beef, yellow onion, dill, ½ teaspoon salt, and ¼ teaspoon pepper and mix together with your hands. Shape into a patty about ¾ inch thick. Do not compact the meat.

In a sauté pan, melt 2 tablespoons of the butter over medium heat. Add the red onion and saute until soft and translucent, about 8 minutes. Add the paprika and cook for about 3 minutes longer. Remove to a plate.

In the same sauté pan, melt the remaining 2 table-spoons butter over high heat. Add the mushrooms and cook, stirring occasionally, until they give off some liquid and shrink down, about 5 minutes. Add the sautéed red onion and the beef stock and bring to a simmer over medium heat. Season to taste with salt and pepper. Keep warm.

Heat a heavy skillet over medium-high heat. Add the beef patty and cook, turning once, for 3 to 4 minutes on each side for medium-rare or until done as desired.

When the burger is ready, stir the sour cream into the mushrooms over low heat and simmer for 1 minute. Transfer the burger to a warmed plate and spoon the mushrooms over the meat.

PORK TENDERLOIN with TWO MARINADES

Pork tenderloin is the ideal cut for a solo diner. You can get one sizable supper out of it and enough to serve alongside a rice salad, some cooked asparagus with ginger vinaigrette, or a potato or lentil salad. The meat is moist and cooks quickly, whether grilled, broiled, or roasted. Marinate it for an hour or two at room temperature or overnight in the refrigerator.

Asian-inspired marinades work well because they contrast with the natural sweetness of the pork and form a caramelized crust on the outside. This first marinade is a longtime favorite. The recipe was given to me by someone I met at a dinner party in Chicago more than forty years ago, so you know it's great if I am still using it. Of course, it has undergone subtle modifications and variations over the years. The second one includes the Middle Eastern accent of pomegranate molasses.

Partner the tenderloin with rice or wild rice and sugar snap peas, snow peas, spinach, green beans, or asparagus. If you like, accompany the pork with Mango Chutney (page 28) or Russian Hot-and-Sweet Mustard (page 29).

Place the pork in a small roasting pan or baking dish. Select a marinade and whisk together all of the ingredients in a small bowl. Pour the marinade over the tenderloin and roll the meat around in the marinade to coat it well. Cover and let stand at room temperature for 1 to 2 hours or for up to overnight in the refrigerator.

Preheat the broiler or prepare a fire in a charcoal grill and broil or grill, turning once, until the meat tests done, about 8 minutes on each side. Alternatively, preheat the oven to 425°F. Roast the pork until an instant-read thermometer inserted into the thickest part registers 140°F, about 25 minutes.

Transfer the pork to a cutting board and let rest for 5 minutes, then slice across the grain.

1 pork tenderloin, 14 to 16 ounces

GINGER and SOY MARINADE

1 or 2 plump cloves garlic, minced (about 1 teaspoon)

3-inch piece fresh ginger, peeled and grated (about 3 tablespoons)

3 tablespoons soy sauce

1 tablespoon tomato paste or 2 tablespoons ketchup

1 tablespoon mild vinegar

3 tablespoons brown sugar

1/2 cup chicken or meat stock

CITRUS and POMEGRANATE MARINADE

1 teaspoon finely minced garlic

1 tablespoon Russian Hot-and-Sweet Mustard or your favorite store-bought brand

2 teaspoons peeled and grated fresh ginger

1 tablespoon soy sauce

1 tablespoon pomegranate molasses, preferably Cortas brand

1 teaspoon grated orange zest

1/2 cup fresh orange juice

LAMB STEAK with GREEK TOMATO SAUCE and FETA

The Greeks have a natural affinity for lamb and a huge repertoire of wonderful recipes using it. I love the way cinnamon, oregano, tomato, and wine come together here, reminiscent of moussaka, but without all the work. Accompany with roasted potatoes and sautéed zucchini or, of course, eggplant.

1 lamb steak, about 8 ounces and 3/4 inch thick, or 3 loin chops, about 12 ounces total

2 teaspoons olive oil

Pinch of ground cinnamon

1/2 teaspoon dried oregano

Freshly ground black pepper

TOMATO SAUCE

2 tablespoons olive oil

1/2 yellow onion, chopped, or 3 or 4 green onions, including tender green tops, chopped

1 teaspoon minced garlic

1/2 teaspoon ground cinnamon

1 teaspoon dried oregano

2/3 cup tomato sauce

1/4 cup meat stock or dry red or white wine

Salt and freshly ground black pepper

Honey or sugar, if needed

1/4 cup crumbled feta cheese

1 tablespoon chopped fresh flat-leaf parsley

Rub the lamb with the olive oil, cinnamon, oregano, and a little pepper. Cover and marinate for 1 or 2 hours at room temperature or overnight in the refrigerator. Bring to room temperature before cooking.

To make the sauce: In a sauté pan, heat the olive oil over medium heat. Add the onion and sauté until soft and translucent, about 8 minutes. Add the garlic, cinnamon, and oregano and cook, stirring occasionally, until tender, about 5 minutes. Add the tomato sauce and stock, bring the mixture to a boil, and then quickly reduce the heat to low. Simmer for 8 minutes to blend the flavors. Season to taste with salt and pepper. Be careful not to oversalt, as the feta cheese will add some saltiness upon final assembly of the dish. Add honey if the tomato sauce tastes acidic.

Preheat the broiler. Broil the lamb steak, turning once, about 4 minutes on each side for medium-rare or until done as desired. Transfer to a warmed dinner plate and spoon the sauce over the top. Garnish with the feta and parsley.

continued

Variation: Instead of broiling the lamb, cook it in 1 tablespoon oil in a heavy skillet over medium heat. Plan on 4 or 5 minutes on each side for medium-rare (depending on thickness) or until done as desired. Remove to a warmed dinner plate, deglaze the pan with ¼ cup meat stock or dry red or white wine, and add the hot tomato sauce. Return the steak to the pan to coat with the sauce, then return to the plate. Top with the feta and parsley.

Easy Lamb Chops

As I have already said, I do not roast a leg of lamb for a solo supper, but I do buy lamb steaks, cross sections cut through the leg, which can be quickly cooked in a skillet and devoured in one sitting. They take to a pan sauce well, too, or are delicious served with Sun Gold Tomato Chutney (page 30).

I also love small lamb rib chops, but they are costly and one or two have so little meat on the bone that I am never satisfied with the portion. In fact, they are so precious, that all I want to do is cook them perfectly and eat them with my fingers. They can be marinated briefly and require no sauce.

Here are four tasty marinades for lamb chops:

Brush the chops with Pomegranate Marinade and Basting Sauce (page 26). Marinate for 1 to 3 hours.

Rub the chops with a mixture of *pimentón de la Vera* (see page 22), ground cumin, and a bit of dried oregano. Marinate for at least 3 hours or for up to overnight.

Rub the chops with a paste of chopped fresh rosemary, minced garlic, red pepper flakes, olive oil, and white wine or fresh lemon juice. Marinate for 1 to 3 hours.

Rub the chops with a Moroccan-inspired paste of ground cumin, paprika, cayenne pepper, minced garlic, and fresh lemon juice, or with Moroccan Charmoula Marinade (page 111). Marinate for at least 2 hours or for up to 1 day.

CALVES' LIVER with ONION and SAGE

I have a weakness for calves' liver. I like it seared very quickly over high heat, crusty and brown on the outside and rather rare in the center. Shades of *Rosemary's Baby*, I know. But I cannot eat it if it is cooked through. My favorite calves' liver recipe is *fegato alla veneziana*, prepared as they do it in Venice, with caramelized onions, sage, and a bit of lemon to lighten the dish. The liver is cut into tiny strips in the Venetian style, but large slices are easier to turn. You have to think ahead if you want it with creamy polenta. The polenta may take twenty minutes, but the liver cooks in just five minutes. If you don't have the patience to stir polenta, you could use instant (I am not crazy about its texture) or accompany the liver with mashed potatoes.

4 tablespoons olive oil

1 red onion, halved and sliced ¼ inch thick

About ¼ cup all-purpose flour

Salt and freshly ground black pepper

6 to 8 ounces calves' liver, well trimmed and sliced about ⅓ inch thick

½ cup chicken stock

2 fresh sage leaves

1 tablespoon fresh lemon juice, or to taste

In a large sauté pan, heat 2 tablespoons olive oil over medium heat. Add the onion and sauté until golden, about 15 minutes. Remove the onion to a plate and set aside.

On a flat plate, stir together the flour with a little salt and pepper. If desired, cut the liver slices into strips ¼ inch wide and 2 inches long. Dredge the liver in the seasoned flour and shake off the excess.

In the same sauté pan, heat the remaining 2 table-spoons oil over high heat. Add the liver and sear, turning once, for 2 to 3 minutes on each side for medium-rare. Remove the liver to a warmed dinner plate and keep warm.

Pour off any excess oil from the pan and return the pan to high heat. Pour in the stock and deglaze the pan, scraping up any browned bits from the pan bottom. Reduce the sauce until slightly thickened. Return the onion to the pan, add the sage leaves and lemon juice, and cook for 2 to 3 minutes. Season with salt and pepper. Spoon the onion over the liver and eat at once.

Desserts

Desserts

Dessert is not one of my daily needs. If I feel I want "dessert," fruit and cheese are the most likely finale to my solo supper. Or just cheese. Sometimes I am happy to nibble on a few berries, some segments of tangerine, or a perfectly ripe pear. When the rare craving for sweets hits, I'm not embarrassed to go out and purchase a pastry. (Alas, my weakness is a chocolate-glazed, custard-filled éclair). I bake or make fancy sweets only when I have company. I won't make a pie or cake just for me, only to have it go bad after a few days, or to binge on it and then have to repent at the gym.

Every once in a while, however, I do make a special dessert for myself, probably because I bought too much fruit at the farmers' market and I don't want to throw it out. So I prepare a fruit gratin or compote with citrus juices. I might make zabaglione or sauté some apple slices with butter and honey, and if I have leftover rice, I sometimes put together a rice pudding—adult baby food for anyone who likes comforting desserts.

ZABAGLIONE

When I went to buy a copper zabaglione pot at Figone Hardware, a North Beach institution now long gone, I talked with the owner about zabaglione, hoping to get a few tips. He told me that he no longer ate it, which I found unusual for an Italian. Then he told me the reason: when he was a little boy, and rather thin and sickly, his mother would make him drink a glass of zabaglione every morning before he went to school. Needless to say, I understood why he couldn't look at it again. This is not my life story, however, so I still crave zabaglione. I have so many happy memories associated with this voluptuous dessert that I actually take the time to make it for myself whenever I am homesick for Italy.

While zabaglione is delicious spooned over berries or ripe peaches, it's really best licked slowly off a spoon. I make it with a whisk or, if feeling lazy, with a small, handheld electric mixer. A double boiler is best, but a small, deep bowl set over a pan of simmering water will also work. A copper zabaglione pot is grand, too, but you do have to polish it from time to time so it doesn't look disreputable.

2 egg yolks

2 tablespoons sugar

¼ cup dry or sweet Marsala

In the top pan of a small double boiler over simmering water, beat together the egg yolks, sugar, and Marsala until they are pale and thick and the whisk or beaters leave tracks when lifted. Do not poop out and stop mixing too soon. It will take about 10 minutes, and it has to be very thick and creamy to be right. It will have doubled in volume. Eat with a spoon while it is warm. Slowly.

STRAWBERRIES with BLOOD ORANGE JUICE

This could not be simpler, and it is a perfect dessert when you want something light and not too sweet. Cut strawberries into thick slices. Sprinkle lightly with sugar and squeeze the juice of 1 blood orange on top. Let macerate for 30 minutes. If blood oranges are not available, try a good squeeze of Meyer lemon juice.

FRUIT GRATIN

A gratin makes familiar fruit seem fancy. Preheat the broiler far enough in advance so that the sugar melts quickly and the fruit doesn't overcook. You can also use a combination of fruits.

1 generous cup strawberries, raspberries, blueberries, or blackberries or 1 large peach or nectarine

⅓ cup sour cream

1 tablespoon milk or half-and-half

1 tablespoon granulated sugar

2 tablespoons brown sugar, or as needed

Preheat the broiler.

If using strawberries, hull them and quarter or halve lengthwise, depending on size. If using a peach, peel and remove the pit, then slice about ½ inch thick. You do not need to peel the nectarine; simply pit and slice. Place the fruit on the bottom of a small flameproof gratin or baking dish.

In a small bowl, whisk together the sour cream, milk, and granulated sugar. Spoon this mixture over the fruit. Sprinkle enough brown sugar over the sour cream to coat it in a thin, even layer. Place the dish under the broiler and broil until the sugar melts. This will happen very quickly, so pay attention to prevent burning. Eat at once.

CHEESE and FRUIT

Pear, Gorgonzola Dolcelatte, and Chestnut Honey:
Peel, core, and slice 1 pear. Arrange the slices atop a slice of
Gorgonzola dolcelatte cheese. Drizzle with dark chestnut
honey. Accompany with toasted walnuts or hazelnuts if a
crunch is desired.

Mascarpone and Chestnuts: Loosely swirl together
½ cup mascarpone cheese and ½ cup sweetened chestnut
purée, or a dollop of mascarpone and a few chopped candied
chestnuts or marrons in syrup. Sweet and sinful.

Cheese with Figs or Quince Paste: Pair fresh or aged
goat's or sheep's milk cheese with fresh or dried figs or with
quince paste. Accompany with walnut bread or wheatmeal
crackers. A traditional Spanish pairing is Manchego cheese and
quince paste, but I also like quince paste with a crottin (aged
goat's milk cheese).

Cheese with Grapes or Apples: Pair Brie, Camembert,
Gruyère, or Morbier cheese with grapes or apple slices.

CREAMY RICE PUDDING

When I was in graduate school at Yale, I sometimes needed a cocktail or a sweet to relax me after spending a long day and night in the painting studio. George and Harry's Pub was near the art school, so I'd meet friends there for an after-work pick-me-up. I usually ordered the kitchen's "famous" rice pudding, but it had no raisins and never enough cinnamon to satisfy me. To compensate, I carried raisins in my pocket so I could "fix" the pudding on the spot. The waiters thought I was eccentric. I guess I was. At home, of course, I can make it just the way I like it. If you have leftover cooked rice, use ½ cup of it to make the pudding and omit the first step of cooking the rice.

1 cup water

Pinch of salt

3 tablespoons short-grain white rice

1 cup milk

2 tablespoons sugar

1 tablespoon unsalted butter

1-inch strip lemon zest

1-inch piece cinnamon stick

2 tablespoons golden raisins

¼ teaspoon vanilla extract

Ground cinnamon for garnish

In a saucepan, bring the water to a boil. Add the salt and rice, reduce the heat to low, and cook, uncovered, until the rice has swelled and is tender, 15 to 20 minutes. Drain the rice and set aside.

In the same saucepan, combine the milk, sugar, butter, lemon zest, and cinnamon stick and bring to a boil. (If you have the time and patience, remove the mixture from the heat at this point and let steep for 30 minutes to develop the flavors.) Add the cooked rice and raisins and simmer slowly, stirring often, until thickened, 10 to 15 minutes. Remove and discard the lemon zest and cinnamon stick and stir in the vanilla. Spoon the pudding into a bowl or eat warm, straight from the pot. In either case, sprinkle with cinnamon.

DESSERT FRENCH TOAST with FRUIT

In Spain, this dessert is called *torrijas* and is served drizzled with a simple syrup. In France, it is called *pain perdu* and is often topped with a compote of sautéed apples. Berries, sautéed peaches, and brandied cherries are other topping options. French toast makes a particularly comforting ending to a light supper, although you might also enjoy it for a solo Sunday brunch.

1 egg

1/3 to 1/2 cup milk

1/4 teaspoon vanilla or almond extract

1 slice firm white bread, such as old-fashioned white, brioche, or challah, about 1 inch thick, crusts removed, and trimmed neatly into a round or square

1/4 cup dried bread crumbs

1/4 teaspoon ground cinnamon

2 teaspoons sugar, plus more to taste

1 1/2 tablespoons unsalted butter, plus more as needed for fruit

1 apple, peach, or banana or 1/3 cup sliced strawberries

Flavorful honey as needed

Crème fraîche for serving

In a shallow bowl, whisk the egg until blended, then whisk in the milk and vanilla extract, using the larger amount of milk if the bread slice is particularly thick. Add the bread and let it stand until it has absorbed all of the liquid. On a plate, stir together the bread crumbs, cinnamon, and 2 teaspoons sugar. Dip the bread slice in the crumb mixture, coating both sides evenly.

In a sauté pan, melt the 1 1/2 tablespoons butter over medium heat. Add the bread and fry, turning once, until golden brown and slightly crusty on both sides, about 6 minutes total. Remove to a warm plate.

If using an apple, halve, core, peel and slice. In a sauté pan melt 1 1/2 tablespoons butter over medium heat. Add the apple slices and sauté, turning as needed, until tender, 4 to 5 minutes. Add honey or sugar to taste.

If using a peach or banana, peel, pit if needed, and slice. Warm 2 tablespoons honey and 1 tablespoon butter over medium heat. Add the fruit and turn the slices in the warm honey-butter mixture for a few minutes, but do not cook them.

Spoon the warmed fruit or strawberries over the bread. Top with a dollop of crème fraîche. Eat warm.

Index

Table of Equivalents

The exact equivalents in the following tables have been rounded for convenience.

LIQUID/DRY MEASURES

U.S.	Metric
¼ teaspoon	1.25 milliliters
½ teaspoon	2.5 milliliters
1 teaspoon	5 milliliters
1 tablespoon (3 teaspoons)	15 milliliters
1 fluid ounce (2 tablespoons)	30 milliliters
¼ cup	60 milliliters
⅓ cup	80 milliliters
½ cup	120 milliliters
1 cup	240 milliliters
1 pint (2 cups)	480 milliliters
1 quart (4 cups, 32 ounces)	960 milliliters
1 gallon (4 quarts)	3.84 liters
1 ounce (by weight)	28 grams
1 pound	454 grams
2.2 pounds	1 kilogram

LENGTH

U.S.	Metric
⅛ inch	3 millimeters
¼ inch	6 millimeters
½ inch	12 millimeters
1 inch	2.5 centimeters

OVEN TEMPERATURE

Fahrenheit	Celsius	Gas
250	120	½
275	140	1
300	150	2
325	160	3
350	180	4
375	190	5
400	200	6
425	220	7
450	230	8
475	240	9
500	260	10